Pr

OUR LORD

WITH

ST. THÉRÈSE
OF LISIEUX

Praying In The Presence Of

Our Lord

WITH

ST. THÉRÈSE
OF LISIEUX

MONICA DODDS

FR. BENEDICT J. GROESCHEL, C.F.R.
SERIES EDITOR

Our Sunday Visitor Publishing Division
Our Sunday Visitor, Inc.
Huntington, Indiana 46750

Nihil Obstat: Rev. Michael Heintz, Censor Librorum
Imprimatur: The Most Rev. John M. D'Arcy
Bishop of Fort Wayne-South Bend
June 25, 2004

The *Nihil Obstat* and *Imprimatur* are official declarations that a book
or pamphlet is free from doctrinal or moral error. It is not implied that
those who have granted the *Nihil Obstat* and *Imprimatur* agree with
the contents, opinions, or statements expressed.

The author and publisher are grateful for permission for excerpts from
Story of a Soul, translated by John Clarke, O.C.D., © 1975, 1976,
1996 by the Washington Province of Discalced Carmelites. ICS
Publications, 2131 Lincoln Road, N.E., Washington, DC 20002-
1199. U.S.A. www.icspublications.org. *St. Thérèse of Lisieux: Her Last
Conversations*, translated by John Clarke, O.C.D., © 1977 by the
Washington Province of Discalced Carmelites. ICS Publications, 2131
Lincoln Road, N.E., Washington, DC 20002-1199. U.S.A.
Scripture citations are taken from the *Catholic Edition of the Revised
Standard Version of the Bible* (RSV), copyright © 1965, 1966 by the
Division of Christian Education of the National Council of Churches
of Christ in the United States of America. Used by permission. All
rights reserved.

ISBN: 1-59276-042-2 (Inventory No. T93)
LCCN: 2003113167

Cover design by Tyler Ottinger
Cover art by Robert F. McGovern
Interior design by Sherri L. Hoffman

PRINTED IN THE UNITED STATES OF AMERICA

DEDICATION

For all the past, present, and future members
of my first parish, St. Thérèse Church, Seattle

Table of Contents

✠

Foreword

✠

Since we began our series on praying to the Eucharist with different saints and well-known spiritual people, we have been obviously waiting for a book on the devotion of St. Thérèse of Lisieux. St. Thérèse's beautiful contribution to Catholic piety, unique enough to have her named a doctor of the Church, is a very personal spirituality of love. St. Thérèse said that her vocation in life was to love.

This totally obscure Carmelite nun known to only a few, who died in her early twenties, left in her autobiography evidence and witness to her profound and total dedication to Our Lord Jesus Christ as well as her devotion to Christ in the Eucharist. It is a joy to recommend this book to our readers. May I suggest that it accompany you often to Eucharistic holy hours and visits to the Blessed Sacrament.

People of the twentieth century greatly profited by the writings and spirituality of St. Thérèse. There is no reason why we should not continue to do so.

FR. BENEDICT J. GROESCHEL, C.F.R.

Introduction

✢

Picture a two-year-old girl living in France in 1875, who one day proudly announces, "I will be a religious." Not "I want to be" but "I will be." Thérèse Martin set her goals early; following in her older sisters' footsteps, she was determined to become a Carmelite nun.

Thérèse was born January 2, 1873, in Alencon, France, to Louis and Zelie Martin. Her parents were very devout Catholics, and they instilled a strong faith in God in their children. Thérèse was the youngest of five girls, (two boys and one girl died as infants and a sister died at the age of five, three years before Thérèse was born). The four older sisters were very gentle and loving to Thérèse, affectionately calling her "baby." The eldest sister, Marie, was thirteen years older than Thérèse. Pauline was twelve years older; followed by Leonie, ten years older; and finally, Celine, only four years older. Celine became a constant companion of Thérèse during her childhood.

Zelie Martin died of breast cancer in 1877 when Thérèse was only four years old. Her sister Pauline took the role as a second mother to Thérèse, and Thérèse's affection for her is evident in her writing. The family moved to Lisieux at this time to have the support of her mother's extended family and to give the girls the opportunity to know their cousins.

Prior to her mother's death, Thérèse, who was frequently described as lively and precocious, became more sullen, private, and introverted, quickly displaying tears. She had a bout with an emotional illness in 1882, with symptoms such as nervous trembling, headaches, insomnia, and hallucinations. On Pentecost Sunday, May 13, 1883, she was cured following a miraculous experience, "seeing" the smiling face of Our Lady.

Years later, Thérèse described what happened:

"Finding no help on earth, poor little Thérèse had also turned towards the Mother of heaven, and prayed with all her heart that she take pity on her. All of the sudden the Blessed Virgin appeared *beautiful* to me, so *beautiful* that never had I seen anything so attractive; her face was suffused with an ineffable benevolence and tenderness, but what penetrated to the very depths of my soul was the *'ravishing smile of the Blessed Virgin.'* At that instant, all my pain disappeared, and two large tears glistened on my eyelashes, and flowed down my cheeks silently, but they were tears of unmixed joy. Ah! I thought, the Blessed Virgin smiled at me, how happy I am."

SS 65-66

Thérèse had always been very close to her father, calling him her "dear King." In 1887 he had an episode of paralysis, and over several years he experienced recurring health problems, including mental illness that led to institutionalization. Louis Martin's suffering caused Thérèse great distress, and she describes him in very loving terms in her writings. He died July 29, 1894.

Throughout her childhood, Thérèse continued her plans to become a Carmelite nun. Each of her sisters had also chosen the religious life. Marie entered Carmel in 1886 and became Sister Marie of the Sacred Heart. Pauline entered in 1882 and took the name Sister Agnes of Jesus. Her sister Leonie chose not to enter Carmel, but instead selected the Visitation order, taking the name, Sister Francoise-Thérèse. Celine entered Carmel but not until after the death of their father, and took the name Sister Genevieve of the Holy Face.

Initially, when Thérèse requested admission to Carmel, the Order refused her because she was too young. However, she was determined not to wait until she was older and petitioned the local bishop (she wore her hair up on top of her head to look more mature) and eventually Pope Leo XIII in Rome (speaking directly to the Pontiff and choosing to ignore the Papal protocol she had been taught), asking for their assistance in persuading the Order to admit her. Both suggested that she wait patiently. Finally in April 1888, while still a mere fifteen years old, Thérèse was accepted into Carmel in Lisieux and received the name "Sister Thérèse of the Child Jesus and the Holy Face."

In 1893, Sister Agnes of Jesus (Pauline) was elected Prioress of the Order and Sister Thérèse was assigned to the spiritual formation of new members of the community. As Prioress, Mother Agnes of Jesus, asked Sister Thérèse to write her memories of her childhood, the family and her intense desire to enter Carmel.

Thérèse hesitated but obeyed:

"I come to confide the story of my soul. The day you asked me to do this, it seemed to me it would distract my heart by too much concentration on myself, but since then Jesus has made me feel that in obeying simply, I would be pleasing Him; besides, I'm going to be doing only one thing: I shall begin to sing what I must sing eternally: '*The Mercies of the Lord.*'"

SS 13

She chose to write her assignment in the form of letters. These memoirs became known as *Manuscript A*.

In September 1896, Sister Marie of the Sacred Heart (Marie) requested that Thérèse write about her "Little Way," a view of how to live a holy life and reach heaven.

Thérèse questioned her ability to explain something so personal:

"I am going to stammer some words even though I feel it is quite impossible for the human tongue to express things which the human heart can hardly understand."

SS 187

The result of this request became *Manuscript B*.

In June 1897, just a few months before Thérèse's death, the new Prioress, Mother Marie de Gonzague, requested that Thérèse write one more assignment, to tell about her life as a Carmelite nun. Thérèse described her life as a cloistered sister, the challenges of community life, and her experiences being responsible for the spiritual formation of the new members of the community. This text included a very private revelation of what Thérèse called her "trial of faith." In her writings she gives an account of the doubts and questions she had about her faith. This "trial" was to continue to plague Thérèse until her death. This final assignment became *Manuscript C*.

The three manuscripts A, B, and C were combined to become Thérèse's autobiography *Story of a Soul* (*SS*). Frequently throughout this autobiography, Thérèse referred to verses of Holy Scripture. Reading the Bible and spending hours in meditation were a large part of her life. Quotes and footnotes were included in her manuscript.

In 1896, Sister Thérèse began to experience the first symptoms of what would be her terminal illness, later diagnosed as tuberculosis. She saw this as the "approach of the Bridegroom" and accepted it as God's will. During the last six months of Thérèse's life, Mother Agnes of Jesus was assigned as her primary caregiver. Mother kept a notebook ("the yellow notebook") near Thérèse's bedside and recorded what Thérèse said. Later, these notes were compiled and published as the *Last Conversation* (*LC*).

Sister Thérèse of the Child Jesus and the Holy Face died near 7:00 pm on September 30, 1897, at the age of twenty-four.

In 1925, only twenty-eight years after her death, Pope Pius XI canonized her St. Thérèse of Lisieux, the Little Flower.

In 1997, on the centennial of her death, Pope John Paul II declared her a Doctor of the Church. In his apostolic letter, "*Divini Amoris Scientia*" ("The Knowledge of Divine Love"), he introduces all of us to this "little saint":

"Shining brightly among the little ones to whom the secrets of the kingdom were revealed in a most special way is Thérèse of the Child Jesus and the Holy Face, a professed nun of the order of Discalced Carmelites …

"Thérèse is a teacher of the spiritual life with a doctrine both spiritual and profound, which she drew from the gospel sources under the guidance of the divine Teacher and then imparted to her brothers and sisters in the church with great effectiveness …

"Despite her inadequate training and lack of resources for studying and interpreting the sacred books, Thérèse immersed herself in meditation on the word of God with exceptional faith and spontaneity. Under the influence of the Holy Spirit she attained a profound knowledge of revelation for herself and for others…

"One can say with conviction about Thérèse of Lisieux that the Spirit of God allowed her heart to reveal directly to the people of our time the fundamental mystery, the reality of the gospel. Her 'little way' is the way of 'holy childhood'."

Because of the popularity of this saint, many books have been written about her, telling her life story, complete with analysis and commentary.

Praying in the Presence of the Lord offers a different focus. Here, in her own words, you will read Thérèse's reflections on her love of God, the way she lived her life, how she approached her death, and her view of eternity.

These selections are from two sources:

1) *Story of a Soul*, Thérèse's autobiography divided into three parts

> Childhood
> The "Little Way"
> Life as a religious

2) *Last Conversations*, a collection of quotes drawn from the meticulous notes kept by her caregiver, Mother Agnes of Jesus, during the last six months of Thérèse's life.

With permission, I have used the translation of Thérèse's writing by John Clarke, O.C.D. While there are other translations, the work by Clarke is the most widely accepted version. Whenever possible I have arranged the quotes in chronological order and have used the same punctuation that Thérèse used, including italics and capital letters. Each quotation is identified by the source. All quotes from *Story of a Soul* are marked as "*SS*" followed by the page numbers. The quotes from *Last Conversations* are labeled as "*LC*," followed by the page number and the date Mother Agnes of Jesus recorded the statement in her notebook.

Thérèse will show us a way to a holy life, her "little way." It is sweet and charming, but we need to remember it is hers, not ours. We cannot try to replicate her way in our lives any more than we can become a twenty-four-year-old Carmelite nun living in France in the late 1800s. Instead, we each need to find our own way, and fortunately, we have Thérèse as a guide. If we get distracted by her story or her quotations, she will quickly re-direct us back to God.

Praying in the Presence of the Lord with St. Thérèse of Lisieux is spending time with God. A time of silence. A time for listening. A time kneeling before Christ in the Blessed Sacrament.

He is waiting for us.

MONICA DODDS

PART

I

Love of . . .

I.

God: Father, Son, and Holy Spirit

✠

COME TO MY WEDDING

(Thérèse's cousin Jeanne Guerin was married on October 1, 1890. After reading the invitation to the wedding, Thérèse decided to write her own wedding invitation.)

"Letter of Invitation to the Wedding of Sister Thérèse of the Child Jesus and the Holy Face.

"God Almighty, Creator of Heaven and Earth, Sovereign Ruler of the Universe, and the Most Glorious Virgin Mary, Queen of the Heavenly Court, announce to you the Spiritual Espousals of Their August Son, Jesus, King of kings, and Lord of lords, with little Thérèse Martin, now Princess and Lady of His Kingdoms of the Holy Childhood and the Passion, assigned to her in dowry by her Divine Spouse, from which Kingdoms she holds her title of nobility — of the Child Jesus and the Holy Face.

"Monsieur Louis Martin, Proprietor and Master of Domains of Suffering and Humiliation, and Madame Martin, Princess and Lady of Honor of the Heavenly Court, wish to have you take part in the Marriage of their Daughter, Thérèse, with Jesus, the Word of God, the Second Person of the Adorable Trinity, Who through the operation of the Holy Spirit was made Man and Son of Mary, Queen of Heaven.

"Being unable to invite you to the Nuptial Blessing, which was given on Mount Carmel, September 8, 1890, (the heavenly court alone was admitted), you are nevertheless asked to be present at the Return from the Wedding which will take place Tomorrow, the Day of Eternity, on which day Jesus, Son of God, will come on the Clouds of Heaven in the splendor of His Majesty, to judge the Living and the Dead.

"The hour being as yet uncertain, you are invited to hold yourselves in readiness and to watch."

SS 168-169

ALL THE JOY OF HEAVEN

(Writing in the third person, describing how she felt at her First Communion.)

"Ah! How sweet was that first kiss of Jesus! It was a kiss of *love*; I *felt* that I *was loved* and I said, "I love You, and I give myself to You forever!" There were no demands made, no struggles, no sacrifices; for a long time now Jesus and poor Thérèse *looked at* and understood each other. That day, it was no longer simply a *look*, it was fusion; they were no longer two. Thérèse had vanished as a drop of water is lost in the immensity of the ocean. Jesus alone remained; He was the Master, the King. Had not Thérèse asked Him to take away her *liberty*, for her *liberty* frightened her? She felt so feeble and fragile that she wanted to be united forever to the divine Strength! Her joy was too great, too deep for her to contain, and tears of consolation soon flowed … all the joy of Heaven having entered my heart, this exiled heart was unable to bear it without shedding tears."

SS 77

Prayer

Oh, my dear Jesus, come to me in the Eucharist and enter my heart. Let me feel true joy in You. Amen.

THE SECOND VISIT

(After receiving communion for the second time.)

"What a sweet memory I have of this second visit of Jesus! My tears flowed again with an ineffable sweetness, and I repeated to myself these words of St. Paul: 'It is no longer I that live, it is Jesus who lives in me!'"

SS 79

Scripture

"I have been crucified with Christ; it is no longer I who live, but Christ who lives in me; and the life I now live in the flesh I live by faith in the Son of God, who loved me and gave himself for me."

GALATIANS 2:20

COME HOLY SPIRIT

(Describing her Confirmation.)

"Ah! how happy my soul was! Like the Apostles, I awaited the Holy Spirit's visit with great happiness in my soul. I rejoiced at the thought of soon being a perfect Christian and especially at that of having eternally on my forehead the mysterious cross the Bishop marks when conferring this sacrament. Finally the happy moment arrived, and I did not experience an impetuous wind at the moment of the Holy Spirit's descent but rather this *light breeze* [small voice] which the prophet Elias heard on Mount Horeb. On that day, I received the strength to *suffer*, for soon afterwards the martyrdom of my soul was about to commence."

SS 80

Scripture

"And he said, 'Go forth, and stand upon the mount before the LORD.*' And behold, the* LORD *passed by, and a great and strong wind rent the mountains, and broke in pieces the rocks before the* LORD, *but the* LORD *was not in the wind; and after the wind an earthquake, but the* LORD *was not in the earthquake; and after the earthquake a fire, but the* LORD *was not in the fire; and after the fire a still small voice. And when Elijah heard it, he wrapped his face in his mantle and went out and stood at the entrance of the cave."*

I KINGS 19:11-13

PREVENTING MY FALL

"I know that without Him, I could have fallen as low as St. Mary Magdalene, and the profound words of Our Lord to Simon resound with a great sweetness in my soul. I know that '*he to whom less is forgiven,* LOVES *less,*' but I also know that Jesus has *forgiven me more* than *St. Mary Magdalene* since He forgave me *in advance* by preventing me from falling. Ah! I wish I could explain what I feel. Here is an example, which will express my thought at least a little. Suppose a cleaver physician's child meets with a stone in his path, which causes him to fall and break a limb. His father comes to him immediately, picks him up lovingly, takes care of his hurt, using all the resources of his profession for this. His child, completely cured, shows his gratitude. This child is no doubt right in loving his father! But I am going to make another comparison. The father, knowing there is a stone in his child's way, hastens ahead of him and removes it but without anyone's seeing him do it. Certainly, this child, the object of his father's tender foresight, but *UNAWARE* of the misfortune from which he was delivered by him, will not thank him and *will love him less* than if he had been cured by him. But if he should come to learn the danger from which he escaped, *will he not love his father more?* Well, I am this child, the object of the *foreseeing love of a Father* who has not sent His Word to save the just, but *sinners.* He wants me *to love* Him because He *has forgiven* me not much but *ALL.* He has not expected me to *love Him much* like Mary Magdalene, but He has willed that I *KNOW* how He has loved me with a love of *unspeakable foresight* in order that now I may love Him unto *folly!*"

SS 83-84

Scripture

"Therefore I tell you, her sins, which are many, are forgiven, for she loved much; but he who is forgiven little, loves little."

LUKE 7:47

"And as he sat at table in the house, behold, many tax collectors and sinners came and sat down with Jesus and his disci-

ples. And when the Pharisees saw this, they said to his disciples, 'Why does your teacher eat with tax collectors and sinners?' But when he heard it, he said, 'Those who are well have no need of a physician, but those who are sick. Go and learn what this means, 'I desire mercy, and not sacrifice.' For I came not to call the righteous, but sinners.'"

MATTHEW 9:10-13

SPEAK TO GOD

"Before the Blessed Sacrament… This was my only consolation, for was not Jesus my *only Friend*? I knew how to speak only to Him; conversations with creatures, even pious conversations, fatigued my soul. I felt it was far more valuable to speak to God than to speak about Him."

SS 87

Prayer
Here I am, Lord. Sitting quietly, closing my mind to all distractions around me, listening … and it may seem like just silence at first. But I know You're here with me. Waiting for me to be ready. Yes, Lord, I'm listening. Come and be with me. Amen.

ONE HOUR OLD

"Christmas … on that luminous *night* which sheds such light on the delights of the Holy Trinity, Jesus, the gentle, *little* Child of only one hour, changed the night of my soul into rays of light. On that *night* when He made Himself subject to *weakness* and suffering for love of me, He made me *strong* and courageous."

SS 97

DIVINE DEW

"One Sunday, looking at a picture of Our Lord on the Cross, I was struck by the blood flowing from one of the divine hands. I felt a great pang of sorrow when thinking this blood was falling to the ground without anyone's hastening to gather it up. I was resolved to remain in spirit at the foot of the Cross and to receive the divine dew. I understood I was then to pour it out upon souls. The cry of Jesus on the Cross sounded continually in my heart: "*I thirst!*" These words ignited within me an unknown and very living fire. I wanted to give my Beloved to drink and I felt myself consumed with *a thirst for souls*. As yet, it was not the souls of priests that attracted me, but those of *great sinners;* I *burned* with the desire to snatch them from the eternal flames."

SS 99

Scripture
"After this Jesus, knowing that all was now finished, said (to fulfill the scripture), 'I thirst.' A bowl full of vinegar stood there; so they put a sponge full of the vinegar on hyssop and held it to his mouth."

JOHN 19:28-29

ETERNAL REWARDS

"All the great truths of religion, the mysteries of eternity, plunged my soul into a state of joy not of this earth. I experienced already what God reserved for those who love Him (not with the eye but with the heart),* and seeing the eternal rewards had no proportion to life's small sacrifices,** I wanted *to love, to love Jesus with a passion*, giving Him a thousand proofs of my love while it was possible. I copied out several passages on perfect love, on the reception God will give His Elect at the moment *He* becomes their Reward, great and eternal, and I repeated over and over the words of love burning in my heart."

SS 102-103

Scripture

* *"But, as it is written, What no eye has seen, nor ear heard, nor the heart of man conceived, what God has prepared for those who love him, God has revealed to us through the Spirit. For the Spirit searches everything, even the depths of God."*

I CORINTHIANS 2:9-10

** *"I consider that the sufferings of this present time are not worth comparing with the glory that is to be revealed to us."*

ROMANS 8:18

THE VEIL

(Describing the spiritual benefits she shared with her sister, Celine.)

"I don't know if I'm mistaken, but it seems to me the out-pourings of our souls were similar to those of St. Monica with her son when, at the port of Ostia, they were lost in ecstasy at the sight of the Creator's marvels! It appears we were receiving graces like those granted to the great saints… God communicates Himself at times in the midst of great splendor or '*gently veiled, under shadows and figures*.' It was in this way He deigned to manifest Himself to our souls, but how *light* and *transparent* the veil was which hid Jesus from our gaze! Doubt was impossible, faith and hope were unnecessary, and *Love* made us find on earth the One whom we were seeking."

SS 104

NOT IN A GOLDEN CIBORIUM

"He gave Himself to me in Holy Communion more frequently than I would have dared hope. I'd taken as a rule of conduct to receive, without missing a single one, the Communions my confessor permitted, allowing him to regulate the number and not asking. At this time in my life, I didn't have the *boldness* I now have, for I'm very sure a soul must tell her confessor the attraction she feels to receive her God. It is not to remain in a golden ciborium that He comes to us *each day* from heaven; it's to find another heaven, infinitely more dear to Him than the first: the heaven of our soul, made to His image, the living temple of the adorable Trinity!"

SS 104

Prayer

Sometimes I'm afraid it is a sin of pride to think that my God would come and be with me. I'm certainly not worthy of this gift. If I tell others they may think I'm crazy, but I know You are here. Because of my faith I feel You near to me. It's true. I welcome You into my heart. Amen.

SECRET INSTRUCTIONS

"When a gardener carefully tends a fruit he wants to ripen before its time, it's not to leave it hanging on a tree but to set it on his table. It was with such intention that Jesus showered His graces so lavishly upon His little flower [Thérèse]. He, who cried out in His mortal life: *'I thank thee, Father, that thou hast hidden these things from the wise and the prudent and revealed them to babes,'* * willed to have His mercy shine out in me. Because I was little and weak He lowered Himself to me, and He instructed me secretly in the *things* of His *love*."

SS 105

Scripture

* *"At that time Jesus declared, 'I thank thee, Father, Lord of heaven and earth, that thou hast hidden these things from the wise and understanding and revealed them to babes.'"*

MATTHEW 11:25

INTIMATE FRIENDS

"But when God stretches out His *hand* to ask, His hand

is never *empty*, and His intimate friends can draw from Him the courage and strength they need."

SS 110

Prayer

To be an intimate friend of Yours, God, and to receive all the courage and strength I need . . . Thank You. Amen.

FOOLISH THOUGHTS

"Above all, I was growing in love for God; I felt within my heart certain aspirations unknown until then, and at times I had veritable transports of love.

One evening, not knowing how to tell Jesus that I loved Him and how much I desired that He be loved and glorified everywhere, I was thinking He would never receive a single act of love from hell; then I said to God that to please Him I would consent to see myself plunged into hell so that He would be loved eternally in that place of blasphemy. I realized this could not give Him glory since He desires only our happiness, but when we love, we experience the need of saying a thousand foolish things; if I talked in this way, it wasn't because heaven did not excite my desire, but because at this time my heaven was none other than Love, and I felt, as did St. Paul, that nothing could separate us from the Divine Being who so ravished me!"*

SS 112

Scripture

* *"For I am sure that neither death, nor life, nor angels, nor principalities, nor things present, nor things to come, nor*

powers, nor height, nor depth, nor anything else in all creation, will be able to separate us from the love of God in Christ Jesus our Lord."

ROMANS 8:38-39

GOD'S HELPER

"God has no need for anyone to carry out His work, I know, but just as He allows a clever gardener to raise rare and delicate plants, giving him the necessary knowledge for this while reserving to Himself the care of making them fruitful, so Jesus wills to be helped in His divine cultivation of souls.

"What would happen were a clumsy gardener not to graft his bushes properly? If he was ignorant of the nature of each and wished to make roses bloom on peach trees? He'd cause the tree to die, which nevertheless had been good and capable of producing fruit. It's in this way one should know from childhood what God asks of souls and second the action of His graces, without either advancing or holding it back. As little birds learn to *sing* by listening to their parents, so children learn the science of the virtues, the sublime *song* of Divine Love from souls responsible for forming them."

SS 113

THE GRANDEUR AND POWER OF GOD

(While traveling by train through Switzerland from Lisieux to Rome.)

"[I saw] the mountains whose summits were lost in the

clouds, its graceful waterfalls gushing forth in a thousand different ways, its deep valleys literally covered with gigantic ferns and scarlet heather. Ah!... how much good these beauties of nature, poured out *in such profusion*, did my soul. They raised it to heaven which was pleased to scatter such masterpieces on a place of exile [earth] destined to last only a day. I hadn't eyes enough to take in everything. Standing by the window I almost lost my breath; I would have liked to be on both sides of the car [train]. When turning to the other side, I beheld landscapes of enchanting beauty, totally different from those under my immediate gaze.

"At times, we were climbing a mountain peak, and at our feet were ravines the depths of which our glance could not possibly fathom. They seemed about to engulf us. A little later, we were passing through a ravishing little village with its graceful cottages and its belfry over which floated immaculately white clouds. There was, farther on, a huge lake gilded by the sun's last rays, its calm waters blending their azure tints with the fires of the setting sun. All this presented to our enraptured gaze the most poetic and enchanting spectacle one could possibly imagine. And at the end of the vast horizon, we perceived mountains whose indistinct contours would have escaped us had not their snowy summits made visible by the sun not come to add one more charm to the beautiful lake which thrilled us so.

"When I saw all these beauties very profound thoughts came to life in my soul. I seemed to understand already the grandeur of God and the marvels of heaven ... I understood how easy it is to become all wrapped up in self, forgetting entirely the sublime goal of one's calling. I said to myself: When … trials come my way … I shall remember what my eyes have seen today. This thought will encourage me and I shall easily forget my own little interests, recalling the grandeur and power of God, this God whom I want to love alone. I shall not have the misfortune of snatching after *straws*, now that '*my HEART HAS AN IDEA of what Jesus has reserved for those who love him.*'"*

SS 125-126

Scripture

* "*But, as it is written, What no eye has seen, nor ear heard, nor the heart of man conceived, what God has prepared for those who love him, God has revealed to us through the Spirit. For the Spirit searches everything, even the depths of God. For what person knows a man's thoughts except the spirit of the man which is in him? So also no one comprehends the thoughts of God except the Spirit of God. Now we have received not the spirit of the world, but the Spirit which is from God, that we might understand the gifts bestowed on us by God. And we impart this in words not taught by human wisdom but taught by the Spirit, interpreting spiritual truths to those who possess the Spirit.*"

I CORINTHIANS 2:9-13

Prayer

So many times I, too, have seen spectacular views of mountains, oceans, and forests and was amazed at Your goodness. Thank You, Father, for this gift You have given to me. Help me to stop more often in the middle of my busy schedule and appreciate all of nature's beauty around me. Your creation is a treasure to behold. Amen.

THE BLOOD OF CHRIST

"And still *peace*, always *peace*, reigned at the bottom of the chalice."

SS 167

PREPARATIONS

"When I am preparing for Holy Communion, I picture my soul as a piece of land and I beg the Blessed Virgin to remove from it *any rubbish* that would prevent it from being *free*; then I ask her to set up a huge tent worthy of *heaven*, adorning it with *her own* jewelry; finally, I invite all the angels and saints to come and conduct a magnificent concert there. It seems to me that when Jesus descends into my heart He is content to find Himself so well received and I, too, am content."

SS 172

THE LOVE OF GOD

"My nature was such that fear made me recoil; with *love* not only did I advance, I actually *flew*."

SS 174

LEAVE EVERYTHING

"God gives the hundredfold in this life to those souls who leave everything for love of Him."*

SS 176

Scripture

* *"Jesus said to them, 'Truly, I say to you, in the new world, when the Son of man shall sit on his glorious throne, you who have followed me will also sit on twelve thrones, judging the twelve tribes of Israel. And every one who has left houses or brothers or sisters or father or mother or children or lands, for my name's sake, will receive a hundredfold, and inherit eternal life. But many that are first will be last, and the last first.'"*

MATTHEW 19:28-30

FOLLY

"And now I have no other desire except *to love* Jesus unto folly."

SS 178

Prayer

To love You, Lord, does not have to be so serious that I can't smile. Amen.

A JUST GOD

"What a sweet joy it is to think that God is *Just*, i.e., that He takes into account our weakness, that He is perfectly aware of our fragile nature. What should I fear? Ah! must not the infinitely just God, who deigns to pardon the faults … of the prodigal son with so much kindness, be just also towards me?"

SS 180

A HOLOCAUST

"O my God! Will Your Justice alone find souls willing to immolate themselves as victims? Does not Your *Merciful Love* need them too? On every side this love is unknown, rejected; those hearts upon whom You would lavish it turn to creatures seeking happiness from them with their miserable affection; they do this instead of throwing themselves into Your arms and accepting Your infinite *Love*. O my God! Is Your distained Love going to remain closed up within Your Heart? It seems to me that if You were to find souls offering themselves as victims of holocaust to Your Love, You would consume them rapidly; it seems to me, too, that You would be happy not to hold back the waves of infinite tenderness within You. If Your Justice loves to release itself, this Justice *which extends only over the earth*, how much more does Your Merciful Love desire to *set souls on fire* since Your Mercy *reaches to the heavens*.* O my Jesus, let me be this happy victim; consume Your holocaust with the fire of Your Divine Love!"

SS 180-181

Scripture
* *"Thy steadfast love, O LORD, extends to the heavens, thy faithfulness to the clouds. Thy righteousness is like the mountains of God, thy judgments are like the great deep; man and beast thou savest, O LORD."*

PSALM 36:5-6

THE FIRE OF LOVE

"On the feast of the Holy Trinity, I received the grace to understand more than ever before how much Jesus desires to be loved … you know the rivers or rather the oceans of graces which [have] flooded my soul! Ah! since that happy day, it seems to me that *Love* penetrates and surrounds me, that at each moment this *Merciful Love* renews me, purifying my soul and leaving no trace of sin within it, and I need have no fear of purgatory. I know that of myself I would not merit even to enter that place of expiation since only holy souls can have entrance there, but I also know that the Fire of Love is more sanctifying than is the fire of purgatory. I know that Jesus cannot desire useless sufferings for us, and that He would not inspire the longings I feel unless He wanted to grant them."

SS 181

GOD ONLY NEEDS LOVE

"See, then, all that Jesus lays claim to from us; He has no need of our works but only of our *love*."

SS 189

GUIDING MY SOUL

"Oh Jesus, my Beloved, who could express the tenderness and sweetness with which You are guiding my soul! It pleases You to cause the rays of Your grace to shine through even in the midst of the darkest storm!"

SS 190

I will face many trials during my lifetime and sometimes I will forget You are here with me. Help me to remember that I always have You as my Guide. Amen.

A VOCATION OF LOVE

"I understood that LOVE COMPRISED ALL VOCA-TIONS, THAT LOVE WAS EVERYTHING, THAT IT EMBRACED ALL TIMES AND PLACES … IN A WORD, THAT IT WAS ETERNAL! Then, in the excess of my delirious joy, I cried out: O Jesus, my Love … my *vocation*, at last I have found it … MY VOCATION IS LOVE!"

SS 194

THE BEACON

"Why speak of a delirious joy? No, this expression is not exact, for it was rather the calm and serene peace of the navigator perceiving the beacon which must lead him to the port … O luminous Beacon of love, I know how to reach You; I have found the secret of possessing Your flame."

SS 195

MY BOLD DESIRES

"Jesus, I cannot fathom the depths of my request; I would be afraid to find myself overwhelmed under the weight of my bold desires … What this child asks for is Love. She knows only one thing; to love You, O Jesus."

SS 196

SONGS OF LOVE

(Thérèse promises to honor God in eternity with flowers.)

"Oh Jesus, of what use will my flowers be to You? Ah! I know very well that this fragrant shower, these fragile, worthless petals, these songs of love from the littlest of hearts will charm You. Yes, these nothings will please You."

SS 197

Prayer

Each time I see a rose, Lord, I will think of the love St. Thérèse had for You. Give me the wisdom to know You and to love You. Amen.

TO POSSESS LOVE

"Jesus, O Jesus, if the *desire* of *loving You* is so delightful, what will it be to possess and enjoy this Love?"

SS 197

MY ASPIRATION

"How can a soul as imperfect as mine aspire to the possession of the plenitude of *Love*? O Jesus, *my first and only Friend*, You whom I *love* UNIQUELY, explain this mystery to me! Why do You not reserve these great aspirations for the great souls!"

SS 197

GIVE ME LIFE

"O Divine Word! You are the Adored Eagle whom I love and who alone *attracts me*! Coming into this land of exile, You willed to suffer and to die in order *to draw* souls to the bosom of the Eternal Fire of the Blessed Trinity. Ascending once again to the Inaccessible Light, henceforth Your abode, You remain still in the 'valley of tears,' hidden beneath the appearances of a white host. Eternal Eagle, You desire to nourish me with Your divine substance and yet I am but a poor little thing who would return to nothingness if Your divine glance did not give me life from one moment to the next."

SS 199

A LEGION OF LITTLE ONES

"But why do I desire to communicate Your secrets of Love, O Jesus, for was it not You alone who taught them to me, and can You not reveal them to others? Yes, I know it, and I beg You to do it. I beg You to cast Your Divine Glance upon a great number of *little* souls. I beg You to choose a legion of *little* Victims worthy of Your LOVE!"

SS 200

Prayer

I know You want the secret of Your love to be shared with everyone. But secrets are hard to explain, Lord. Help me to say the right things, use the right words, express the right thoughts when I try to spread Your message. Help me especially when I meet others who seem to doubt Your presence or even Your existence. Amen.

TO HEAR HIS FIRST CALL

"Ah! my soul was filled with a great consolation; I was interiorly persuaded that Jesus, on the anniversary of His own death, wanted to have me hear His first call [first symptoms of her illness]. *It was like a sweet and distant murmur which announced the Bridegroom's arrival.*"

SS 211

LOVE ATTRACTS LOVE

"O my God, I have never desired anything but to *love* You, and I am ambitious for no other glory. Your Love has gone before me, and it has grown with me, and now it is an abyss whose depths I cannot fathom. Love attracts love, and, my Jesus, my love leaps towards Yours; it would be like to fill the abyss which attracts it, but alas! it is not even like a drop of dew lost in the ocean! For me to love You as You love me, I would have to borrow Your own Love, and then only would I be at rest. O my Jesus, it is perhaps an illusion but it seems to me that You cannot fill a soul with more love than the love with which You have filled mine; it is for this reason that I dare to ask You '*to love those whom you have given me with the love with which you loved me.*'"*

SS 256

Scripture
* "*The glory which thou hast given me I have given to them, that they may be one even as we are one, I in them and thou in me, that they may become perfectly one, so that the world*

may know that thou hast sent me and hast loved them even as thou hast loved me. Father, I desire that they also, whom thou hast given me, may be with me where I am, to behold my glory which thou hast given me in thy love for me before the foundation of the world."

JOHN 17:22-24

DRAW ME

"'*No man can come after me, unless the FATHER who sent me draw[s] him,*'* Jesus has said … Through beautiful parables, and often even without using this means so well known to the people, He teaches us that it is enough to knock and it will be opened, to seek in order to find, and to hold out one's hand humbly to receive what is asked for.** He also says that everything we ask the *Father in His name*, He will grant it.*** No doubt, it is because of this teaching that the Holy Spirit, before Jesus' birth, dictated this prophetic prayer: '*Draw me*'…this is my prayer. I ask Jesus to draw me into the flames of His love, to unite me so closely to Him that He live and act in me. I feel that the more the fire of love burns within my heart, the more I shall say: 'Draw me.'"

SS 257

Scripture
* "*No one can come to me unless the Father who sent me draws him; and I will raise him up at the last day.*"

JOHN 6:44

** *"For everyone who asks receives, and he who seeks finds, and to him who knocks it will be opened."*

MATTHEW 7:8

*** *"In that day you will ask nothing of me. Truly, truly, I say to you, if you ask anything of the Father, he will give it to you in my name. Hitherto you have asked nothing in my name; ask, and you will receive, that your joy may be full."*

JOHN 16:23-24

THE PERFUME

"Since Jesus has re-ascended into heaven, I can follow Him only in the traces He has left; but how luminous these traces are! how perfumed! I have only to cast a glance in the Gospels and immediately I breathe in the perfumes of Jesus' life,… I don't hasten to the first place but to the last; rather than advance like the Pharisee, I repeat, filled with confidence, the publican's humble prayer."

SS 258

UNDER HIS WINGS

(Explaining why she began to cry after watching a mother bird protecting her chicks.)

"I cried when I thought how God used this image in order to teach us His tenderness towards us.* All through my life, this is what He has done for me! He has hidden me totally under His wings! Earlier in the day, when I was leaving you, I was crying when going upstairs; I was

unable to control myself any longer, and I hastened to our cell. My heart was overflowing with love and gratitude."
LC 60 6/7

Scripture

* "O Jerusalem, Jerusalem, killing the prophets and stoning those who are sent to you! How often would I have gathered your children together as a hen gathers her brood under her wings, and you would not! Behold, your house is forsaken and desolate. For I tell you, you will not see me again, until you say, 'Blessed is he who comes in the name of the Lord.'"

MATTHEW 23:37-39

Prayer

Thank You, God, for all You have done for me. Sometimes I am not as able as St. Thérèse to express my feelings. Help me open my heart to understand the depth of Your love for me. Amen.

ON FIRE

"I was beginning the Way of the Cross; suddenly, I was seized with such a violent love for God that I can't explain it except by saying it felt as though I were totally plunged into fire. Oh! What fire and what sweetness at one and the same time! I was on fire with love, and I felt that one minute more, one second more, and I wouldn't be able to sustain this ardor without dying. I understood, then, what the saints were saying about these states which they experienced so often. As for me, I experienced it only once and for one single instant, falling back immediately into my habitual state of dryness…"

"At the age of fourteen, I also experienced transports of love. Ah! how I loved God! But it wasn't at all as it was after my Oblation to Love; it wasn't a real flame that was burning me."

LC 77 7/7

[See "Act of Oblation to Merciful Love"
in appendix of this book, p. 152]

MIRROR OF THE SOUL

(Looking at a picture of the Holy Face of Jesus.)

"How well Our Lord did to lower His eyes when He gave us His portrait! Since the eyes are the mirror of the soul, if we had seen His soul, we would have died from joy."

LC 134 8/5

THE HEAVENS

(A caregiver saw Thérèse gazing at the sky and said:"You look up at the heavens with so much love!" Thérèse simply smiled; but later explained.)

"Ah! she believed I was looking at the sky and thinking of the real heavens! No, it was simply because I admire the material heavens; the other is closed against me more and more. Then immediately I said to myself with great gentleness: Oh, certainly, it's really through love that I'm looking up at the sky; yes, it's through love for God, since everything that I do, my actions, my looks, everything, since my Offering, is done through love."

LC 141 8/8

Prayer

Blessed be the heavens now as I see them with my eyes and in eternity when I share my life with You, God Almighty. Amen.

THE CONFITEOR

"… how great the grace is that I received this morning when the priest began the Confiteor before giving me Communion, and all the Sisters continued. I saw Jesus very close to giving Himself to me, and this confession appears to me as such a necessary humiliation. 'I confess to Almighty God, to Blessed Virgin Mary, to all the saints, that I have sinned exceedingly …' Oh! yes, I said to myself, they do well to beg pardon from God and all the saints for me at this moment … Like the publican, I felt I was a great sinner. I found God to be so merciful! I found it so touching to address oneself to the whole heavenly court to obtain God's pardon through its intercession. Ah! I could hardly keep from crying, and when the Sacred Host touched my lips, I was really moved.

"How extraordinary it is to have experienced this at the Confiteor! I believe it's because of my present disposition; I feel so miserable! [due to her illness] My confidence is not lessened, on the contrary; and the word 'miserable' is not exact, because I am rich with all the divine treasures; but it's exactly because of this that I humble myself even more. When I think of all the graces God gave me, I restrain myself so as not to shed tears of gratitude continually.

"I believe the tears I shed this morning were tears of perfect contrition. Ah! how impossible it is to give oneself such sentiments! It is the Holy Spirit, who gives them, He who 'breathes where he wills.'"*

LC 147 8/12

Scripture

* *"Jesus answered, 'Truly, truly, I say to you, unless one is born of water and the Spirit, he cannot enter the kingdom of God. That which is born of the flesh is flesh, and that which is born of the Spirit is spirit. Do not marvel that I said to you, "You must be born anew." The wind blows where it wills, and you hear the sound of it, but you do not know whence it comes or whither it goes; so it is with every one who is born of the Spirit.'"*

JOHN 3:5-8

Prayer

Confiteor
I confess to almighty God,
and to you, my brothers and sisters,
that I have sinned through my own fault
in my thoughts and in my words,
in what I have done,
and in what I have failed to do;
and I ask blessed Mary, ever virgin,
all the angels and saints,
and you, my brothers and sisters,
to pray for me to the Lord our God.

NO LONGER SUFFERING

(After looking at a crucifix with the head of Our Lord inclined.)

"He is dead. I prefer when they represent Him as dead, because then I think He is no longer suffering."

LC 154 8/19

Prayer

After reading Thérèse's words, there is no doubt of her love for You, dear Lord. She was able to give herself completely to You because of that love. I say "I love you" to people in my life but my love for You is different, deeper, more life-changing. The love I feel in this world is only a glimpse of what awaits me for eternity. Your eternal love for me has always been there and will continue long past my limited time on this earth. I love You. How can I show my love to You? Here I am, Lord, kneeling in Your presence. Amen.

2.
Mary and the Holy Family

✠

Prayer
Hail Mary

Hail Mary, full of grace. The Lord is with thee. Blessed art thou among women, and blessed is the fruit of thy womb, Jesus.

Holy Mary, Mother of God, pray for us sinners, now and at the hour of our death. Amen.

INTO THE ARMS OF MY MOTHER

"In the afternoon, it was I who made the Act of Consecration to the Blessed Virgin. It was only right that I *speak* in the name of my companions to my Mother in heaven, I who had been deprived at such an early age of my earthly Mother. I put all my heart into *speaking* to her, into consecrating myself to her as a child throwing itself into the arms of its mother, asking her to watch over her. It seems to me the Blessed Virgin must have looked upon her little flower [Thérèse] and *smiled* at her, for wasn't it she who cured her with a *visible smile*? Had she not placed in the heart of her little flower her Jesus, the Flower of the Fields and the Lily of the valley?"

SS 78

OUR LADY OF VICTORIES

"Ah! what I felt kneeling at her feet cannot be expressed. The graces she granted me so moved me that my happiness found expression only in tears, just as on the day of my First Communion. The Blessed Virgin made me feel *it was really herself who smiled on me and brought about my cure*. I understood she was watching over me, that I was *her* child. I could no longer give her any other name but "Mamma," as this appeared ever so much more tender than "Mother." How fervently I begged her to protect me always, to bring to fruition as quickly as possible my dream of hiding *beneath the shadow of her virginal mantle!* This was one of my first desires as a child. When growing up, I understood it was at Carmel I would truly find the Blessed Virgin's mantle, and towards this fertile Mount I directed all my desires.

"I prayed Our Lady of Victories to keep far from me everything that could tarnish my purity."

SS 123

Prayer

Mamma, I love you. Amen.

PROTECTION

"I also prayed to St. Joseph, asking him to watch over me, ever since my childhood I had a devotion for him which easily merged with my love for the Blessed Virgin. I recited each day the prayer in his honor: 'St. Joseph, father and guardian of virgins, [into whose faithful keeping were

entrusted Innocence itself, Christ Jesus, and Mary, the Virgin of virgins, I pray and beseech thee through Jesus and Mary, those pledges so dear to thee, to keep me from all uncleanness, and to grant that my mind may be untainted, my heart pure and my body chaste; help me always to serve Jesus and Mary in perfect chastity. Amen.']
And so it was without any fear I understood the long journey; being so well protected; what was there to fear?"

SS 124

OUR LADY'S SUFFERING

"When I was looking at the statue of the Blessed Virgin this evening … I understood that she suffered not only in soul but also in body. She suffered a lot on her journeys from the cold, the heat, and from fatigue. She fasted very frequently.

"Yes, she knew what it was to suffer."

LC 158 8/20

AN IMAGE OF THE HOLY FAMILY

"How charming it will be in heaven to know everything that took place in the Holy Family! When little Jesus began to grow up, perhaps when He saw the Blessed Virgin fasting, He said to her; 'I would really like to fast, too.' And the Blessed Virgin answered: 'No, little Jesus, You are still too little, You haven't the strength.' Or else perhaps she didn't dare hinder Him from doing this.

"And good St. Joseph! Oh! how I love him! He wasn't able to fast because of his work.

"I can see him planing, then drying his forehead from time to time. Oh! how I pity him! It seems to me that their life was simple.

"The country women came to speak familiarly with the Blessed Virgin. Sometimes they asked her to entrust her little Jesus to them so that He would go and play with their children. And little Jesus looked at the Blessed Virgin to see if He should go and play. At times, the good women went directly to the Child Jesus and said to Him quite simply: 'Come and play with my little boy.'

"What does me a lot of good when I think of the Holy Family is to imagine a life that was very ordinary. It wasn't everything that they have told us or imagined. For example, that the Child Jesus, after having formed some birds out of clay, breathed upon them and gave them life. Ah! no! little Jesus didn't perform useless miracles like that, even to please His Mother. Why weren't they transported into Egypt by a miracle which would have been necessary and so easy for God? In the twinkling of an eye, they could been brought there. No, everything in their life was done just as in our own.

"How many troubles, disappointments! How many times did others make complaints to good St. Joseph! How many times did they refuse to pay him for his work! Oh! How astonished we would be if we only knew how much they had suffered!"

LC 159 8/20

Prayer

Dear Mary, it's hard for me to imagine your life as a family, living the day-in-and-day-out experience all families share. But you had a Son

whom you knew was the Savior, the Messiah, that everyone was wait-
ing for. How did you manage when the Son of God was part of your
little family? I pray for all families, that Jesus is a part of their lives.
Amen.

A SERMON ABOUT MARY

"How I would have loved to be a priest in order to preach about the Blessed Virgin! One sermon would be suffi-cient to say everything I think about this subject.

"I'd first make people understand how little is known about her life.

"We shouldn't say unlikely things or things we don't know anything about! For example, that when she was lit-tle, at the age of three, the Blessed Virgin went up to the Temple to offer herself to God, burning with sentiments of love and extraordinary fervor. While perhaps she went there very simply out of obedience to her parents.

"Again, why say, with reference to the aged Simeon's prophetic words, that the Blessed Virgin had the Passion of Jesus constantly before her mind from that moment onward? 'And a sword will pierce through your soul, also,' the old man said.* It wasn't for the present, you see … it was a general prediction for the future.

"For a sermon on the Blessed Virgin to please me and do me any good, I must see her real life, not her imagined life. I'm sure that her real life was very simple. They show her to us as unapproachable, but they should present her as imitable, bringing out her virtues, saying that she lived by faith just like ourselves, giving proofs of this from the Gospel, where we read: 'And they did not understand the words which He spoke to them.'** And that other no less mysterious statement: 'His father and mother marveled at what was said about him.'* This admiration presupposes a certain surprise, don't you think so...?

"We know very well that the Blessed Virgin is Queen of heaven and earth, but she is more Mother than Queen; and we should not say, on account of her prerogatives, that she surpasses all saints in glory just as the sun at its rising makes the stars disappear from sight. My God! How strange that would be! A mother who makes her children's glory vanish! I myself think just the contrary. I believe she'll increase the splendor of the elect very much.

"It's good to speak about her prerogatives, but we should not stop at this, and if, in a sermon, we are obliged from the beginning to end to exclaim and say: Ah! Ah!, we would grow tired! Who knows whether some soul would not reach the point of feeling a certain estrangement from a creature so superior and would not say: If things are such, it's better to go and shine as well as one is able in some little corner!

"What the Blessed Virgin has more than we have is the privilege of not being able to sin, she was exempt from the stain of original sin; but on the other hand, she wasn't as fortunate as we are, since she didn't have a Blessed Virgin to love. And this is one more sweetness for us and one less sweetness for her!"

LC 161-162 8/21

Scripture

* *"And his father and his mother marveled at what was said about him; and Simeon blessed them and said to Mary his*

mother, 'Behold, this child is set for the fall and rising of many in Israel, and for a sign that is spoken against (and a sword will pierce through your own soul also), that thoughts out of many hearts may be revealed.'"

LUKE 2:33-35

** *"And he said to them, 'How is it that you sought me? Did you not know that I must be in my Father's house?' And they did not understand the saying which he spoke to them. And he went down with them and came to Nazareth, and was obedient to them; and his mother kept all these things in her heart."*

LUKE 2:49-51

COMPLAINING

(A comment was made that when she was silent, maybe that meant she was suffering less.)

"Oh! just the opposite! I suffer very much, very much! But it's to the Blessed Virgin that I complained."

LC 184 9/5

Prayer

My Blessed Lady, come to me. I want to feel the warmth of a Mother, holding me, sheltering me, keeping me safe. Thank you for making your brave decision to say "Yes" to God when He asked you to do what seemed to be impossible. You want us to realize how much God loves us. Join me as I pray for peace, you who are the Queen of Heaven. Amen.

3.
The Saints

✠

PEOPLE IN HEAVEN

"O Jesus, the storm was no longer raging, heaven was calm and serene, I *believed*, I *felt* there was a *heaven* and that this *heaven* is peopled with souls who actually love me, who consider me their child."

SS 191

HOLY SAINTS, ADOPT ME

"I presented myself before the angels and saints and I said to them: 'I am the smallest of creatures; I know my misery and my feebleness, but I know also how much noble and generous hearts love to do good. I beg you then, O Blessed Inhabitants of heaven, I beg you to ADOPT ME AS YOUR CHILD.'"

SS 195-196

THE WELCOMING BY THE SAINTS

(After watching a procession of religious in white mantles.)

"I said to myself: This is the way in which the saints know me, love me, and smile upon me from above, inviting me to join them!

"Then the tears came. It has been years since I cried as much as I did then. Ah! but these were tears of consolation!"

LC 49-50 5/26

Prayer

Good Saints, hear my prayer. You have already seen the glorious life that waits for me in heaven. I know you found it beyond anything you might have dreamed of here on earth. You made it, you succeeded. Please help me as I struggle in my journey. Pray for me to our Merciful Father. I look forward to meeting all of you in heaven. Amen.

TO KNOW THE SAINTS

"Oh, I would like to know the story of all the saints in heaven; however, nobody will have to tell it to me as it would take too long. When approaching a saint, I'll … know his name and his whole life in one single glance."

LC 105 7/21

ENCOURAGED BY THE SAINTS

(Looking at a picture of Joan of Arc in prison.)

"The saints encourage me, too, in my prison. They tell me: As long as you are in irons, you cannot carry out your mission; but later on, after your death, this will be the time for your works and your conquests."

LC 144 8/10

Prayer

A Litany of the Saints

Lord, have mercy.   **R**: *Lord, have mercy.*

Christ have mercy.   **R**: *Christ have mercy.*

Lord, have mercy.   **R**: *Lord, have mercy.*

Holy Mary Mother of God,   **R**: *Pray for us.*

Holy angels of God, …

Abraham, our father in faith, …

David, leader of God's people, …

All holy patriarchs and prophets, …

Saint John the Baptist, …

Saint Joseph, …

Saint Thérèse of Lisieux, …

(others saints may be included here)

All holy men and women, …

Christ, hear us.   **R**: *Christ, hear us.*

Lord Jesus, hear our prayer.   **R**: *Lord Jesus, hear our prayer.*

Amen.

PART

II

Life

I.
View of Life

✠

THE SOULS IN JESUS' GARDEN

"I wondered for a long time why God has preferences, why all souls don't receive an equal amount of graces … Jesus deigned to teach me this mystery. He set before me the book of nature; I understood how all the flowers He has created are beautiful, how the splendor of the rose and the whiteness of the Lily do not take away the perfume of the little violet or the delightful simplicity of the daisy. I understood that if all flowers wanted to be roses, nature would lose her springtime beauty, and the fields would no longer be decked out with little wild flowers.

"And so it is in the world of souls, Jesus' garden. He willed to create great souls comparable to lilies and roses, but He has created small ones and these must be content to be daisies or violets destined to give joy to God's glances when He looks down at His feet. Perfection consists in doing His will, in being what He wills us to be.

"I understood, too, that Our Lord's love is revealed as perfectly in the most simple soul that resists His grace in nothing as in the most excellent soul: in fact, since the nature of love is to humble oneself, if all souls resembled those of the holy Doctors who illumined the Church with the clarity of their teachings, it seems God would not descend so low when coming to their heart. But He created the child who knows only how to make his feeble cries heard; He has created a poor savage who has nothing but the natural law to guide him. It is to their hearts that God deigns to lower Himself. These are the wild flowers whose simplicity attracts Him. When coming down in this way, God manifests His infinite grandeur. Just as the sun shines simultaneously on the tall cedars and on each little flower as though it were alone on the earth, so Our Lord is occupied particularly with each soul as though there were no others like it. And just as in nature all the seasons are arranged in such a way as to make the humblest daisy bloom on a set day, in the same way, everything works out for the good of each soul."

SS 13-15

Prayer

God, I love the fragrance of this garden You created. Please help me to understand that I don't have to compete with any of the other "flowers" for Your love. Let me focus all my energy on You. Give me the wisdom to strive to be close to You. Continue to shine Your light on me. Amen.

DIVINE GLANCES

(Thérèse writing in third person.)

"She knows that nothing in herself was capable of attracting the divine glances, and His mercy alone brought about everything that is good in her."

SS 15

TO BECOME A SAINT

"Perfection ... I understood that to become a *saint* one had to suffer much, seek out always the most perfect thing to do, and forget self."

SS 27

DON'T WANDER AWAY

"I made the resolution never to wander far away from the glance of Jesus in order to travel peacefully towards the eternal shore [heaven]!"

SS 49

HIDE YOURSELF

"God made me feel that true glory is that which will last eternally, and to reach it, it isn't necessary to perform striking works but to hide oneself and practice virtue in such a way that the left hand knows not what the right hand is doing." *

SS 72

Scripture
* *"But when you give alms, do not let your left hand know what your right hand is doing, so that your alms may be in secret; and your Father who sees in secret will reward you."*

MATTHEW 6:3-4

THE ONLY GOOD

"And I see that all is vanity and vexation of spirit under the sun,* that the *only good* is to love God with all one's heart and to be *poor in spirit* here on earth."

SS 73

Scripture

* "*Then I considered all that my hands had done and the toil I had spent in doing it, and behold, all was vanity and a striving after wind, and there was nothing to be gained under the sun.*"

ECCLESIASTES 2:11

SPIRITUAL THOUGHTS

"There are certain things that lose their perfume as soon as they are exposed to the air; there are deep *spiritual thoughts* which cannot be expressed in human language without losing their intimate and heavenly meaning; they are similar to '… *the white stone I will give to him who conquers, with a name written on the stone which no one KNOWS except HIM who receives it.*'*"

SS 77

Scripture

* "*He who has an ear, let him hear what the Spirit says to the churches. To him who conquers I will give some of the hidden manna, and I will give him a white stone, with a new name written on the stone which no one knows except him who receives it.*"

REVELATION 2:17

DRAWN FROM THE WORLD

"Oh! how I pity souls that are lost! It is so easy to go astray on the flowery paths of the world. Undoubtedly, for a soul a little advanced spiritually, the sweetness which the world offers is mixed with bitterness, and the *immense* void of the *desires* cannot be filled by the praises of an instant … Did He not, according to the words of Wisdom: '… *draw me from the world before my spirit was corrupted by its malice and before its deceitful appearances has seduced my soul*'?"*

SS 86

Scripture
* "*There was one who pleased God and was loved by him, and while living among sinners he was taken up. He was caught up lest evil change his understanding or guile deceive his soul. For the fascination of wickedness obscures what is good.*"

WISDOM 4:10-12

STILL IMPERFECT

"Although God showered His graces upon me, it wasn't because I merited them because I was still very imperfect. I had a great desire, it is true, to practice virtue."

SS 97

Prayer
Most Holy Spirit, pour Your graces on me and teach me Your virtues. I know this is the way to a holy life. Amen.

TO BE A PRISONER

"Ah! what poetry flooded my soul at the sight of all these things [views while traveling from Italy to France] I was seeing for the first and last time in my life! It was without regret I saw them disappear, for my heart longed for other marvels. It had contemplated *earthly beauties* long enough; *those of heaven* were the object of its desires and to win them for *souls* I was willing to become a *prisoner* [enter Carmel as a cloistered sister]!"

SS 141

TO BE FORGOTTEN

"He whose Kingdom is not of this world* showed me that true wisdom consists in 'desiring to be unknown and counted as nothing,' in 'placing one's joy in the contempt of self.' Ah! I desired that, like the Face of Jesus, 'my face be truly hidden, that no one on earth would know me.'** I thirsted after suffering and I longed to be forgotten."

SS 152

Scripture

* "*Pilate answered, 'Am I a Jew? Your own nation and the chief priests have handed you over to me; what have you done?' Jesus answered, 'My kingship is not of this world; if my kingship were of this world, my servants would fight, that I might not be handed over to the Jews; but my kingship is not from the world.' Pilate said to him, 'So you are a king?' Jesus answered, 'You say that I am a king. For this I was born, and*

for this I have come into the world, to bear witness to the truth. Every one who is of the truth hears my voice.'"

JOHN 18:35-37

"He was despised and rejected by men; a man of sorrows, and acquainted with grief; and as one from whom men hide their faces he was despised, and we esteemed him not."

ISAIAH 53:3

THE DESIRE FOR SOMETHING

"How merciful is the way God has guided me. *Never* has He given me the desire for anything which He has not given me, and even His bitter chalice seemed delightful to me."

SS 152

LITTLE BY LITTLE

"… with regard to the Vow of Poverty. During my postulancy [first year in Carmelite community], I was content to have nice things for my use and to have everything necessary for me at my disposal. 'My *Director* [God] bore this patiently, for He doesn't like pointing everything out at once to souls. He generally gives His light little by little.'"

SS 158

Prayer

My dear "Director," I'm not a fast learner. I may need to hear Your message many times. I want to understand it and make You part of my life. Please don't give up on me. Amen.

HIDE YOURSELF

"I recognized from EXPERIENCE that happiness consists in hiding oneself, in remaining ignorant of created things. I understood that without *love* all works are nothing, even the most dazzling."

SS 175

LOVE CONSUMES EVERYTHING

"How sweet is the way of *love* ... True, one can fall or commit infidelities, but, knowing *how to draw profit from everything*, love quickly consumes everything that can be displeasing to Jesus; it leaves nothing but a humble and profound peace in the depths of the heart."

SS 179

Prayer

Father, forgive me my sins. I have failed so many times. Your forgiveness is a mere glimpse of Your everlasting love for me. Give me Your peace. Amen.

SCRIPTURE

"... the Gospels ... sustain me during my hours of prayer, for in them I find what is necessary for my poor little soul. I am constantly discovering in them new lights, hidden and mysterious meanings."

SS 179

NO NOISE OF WORDS

"I understand and I know from experience that: '*The kingdom of God is within you.*'* Jesus has no need of books and teachers to instruct souls; He teaches without the noise of words. Never have I heard Him speak, but I feel that He is within me at each moment; He is guiding and inspiring me with what I must say and do."

SS 179

Scripture
* "*Being asked by the Pharisees when the kingdom of God was coming, he answered them, 'The kingdom of God is not coming with signs to be observed; nor will they say, 'Lo, here it is!' or 'There!' for behold, the kingdom of God is in the midst of you.'*"

Luke 17:20-21

Prayer
Right here, right now. You are with me today. Wherever I am, whatever I'm doing, no matter the time, You are with me. Always ready to speak to me. Yes, Lord, I'm listening. Amen.

NOT IN BOOKS

"Without showing Himself, without making His voice heard, Jesus teaches me in secret; it is not by means of books, for I do not understand what I am reading. Sometimes a word comes to console me."

SS 187

COMFORT

(Thérèse quoting Isaiah and writing in third person.)

"[Isaiah] … cried out in the Lord's name: *'As one whom a mother caresses, so will I comfort you; you shall be carried at the breast and upon the knees they will caress you.'*

"After having listened to words such as these … there is nothing to do but to be silent and to weep with gratitude and love. Ah! if all weak and imperfect souls felt what the least of souls feel, that is, the soul of your little Thérèse, not one would despair of reaching the summit of the mount of love. Jesus does not demand great actions from us but simply *surrender* and *gratitude*."

SS 188

THE CHURCH

"Considering the mystical body of the Church, I had not recognized myself in any of the members described by St. Paul, or rather I desired to see myself in them *all. Charity* gave me the key to my *vocation.* I understood that if the Church had a body composed of different members, the most necessary and most noble of all could not be lacking to it, and so I understood that the Church *had a Heart and that this Heart* was *BURNING WITH LOVE. I understood it was Love alone* that made the Church's members act, that if *Love* ever became extinct, apostles would not preach the Gospel and martyrs would not shed their blood."

SS 194

Prayer

For the most Holy Church and for each and every member, I pray to the Lord. Amen.

FLOWERS BEFORE THE THRONE

"Yes, my Beloved, this is how my life will be consumed. I have no other means of proving my love for you other than that of strewing flowers, that is, not allowing one little sacrifice to escape, not one look, one word, profiting by all the smallest things and doing them through love. I desire to suffer for love and even to rejoice through love; and in this way I shall strew flowers before Your throne. I shall not come upon one without *unpetalling* it for You. While I am strewing my flowers, I shall sing, for could one cry while doing such a joyous action? I shall sing even when I must gather my flowers in the midst of thorns, and my song will be all the more melodious in proportion to the length and sharpness of the thorns."

SS 196-197

MY HEART TO GOD

"When the human heart gives itself to God, it loses nothing of its innate tenderness; in fact, this tenderness grows when it becomes more pure and more divine."

SS 216

TEACHINGS OF JESUS

"Ah! how contrary are the teachings of Jesus to the feelings of nature! Without the help of His grace it would be impossible not only to put them into practice but to even understand them."

SS 229

Prayer

Jesus, You have challenged me to live a life that, at times, seems impossible. The world and its distractions are all around me. I know I can't do this alone. Please give me the graces I need. Amen.

TO DO GOOD

"One feels that to do good is as impossible without God's help as to make the sun shine at night."

SS 238

INVINCIBLE WEAPONS

"Ah! it is prayer, it is sacrifices which give me all my strength; these are the invincible weapons which Jesus has given me. They can touch souls much better than words as I have very frequently experienced."

SS 241

SPECIAL GRACES AND LIGHTS

"We can say, without any boasting, that we have received very special graces and lights; we stand in the truth and see things in their proper light."

LC 42 5/9

BEGIN AGAIN

(When asked what she would do differently, if she could begin her life again.)

"I would do exactly what I did."   *LC 237 7/12*

BE HUMBLE

(If you feel you are no longer able to think.)

"This doesn't matter, God knows your intentions. As long as you're humble you will be happy."

LC 261 JULY

AN INSTRUMENT

(After hearing that she was fortunate in having been chosen by God to tell souls about the way of confidence.)

"What does it matter whether it's I or someone else who gives this way to souls; as long as the way is pointed out; the instrument is unimportant."

LC 105 7/ 21

HE'S GIVING TO ME

"I look at the grapes, and I say to myself: They are beautiful, they look good. Then I eat one; I don't give this one to Jesus, because He's the one giving it to me."

LC I 10 7/25

Prayer
Thank You, Jesus, for all the things You give me each day. Amen.

IMPERFECTION

"I experience a very living joy not only when I discover I'm imperfect, but especially when I feel I am. All this surpasses all praise, which only bores me."

LC 129 8/2

FORGET MYSELF

(When asked "What did you do to reach such unchangeable peace?")

"I forgot self, and I was careful to seek myself in nothing."

LC 129 8/3

ST. PETER

"I understand very well why St. Peter fell.* Poor Peter, he was relying upon himself instead of relying only upon God's strength. I conclude from this experience that if I said to myself: 'O my God, You know very well I love You too much to dwell upon one single thought against the faith,' my temptations would become more violent and I would certainly succumb to them.

"I'm sure that if St. Peter had said humbly to Jesus: 'Give me the grace, I beg You, to follow You even to death,' he would have received it immediately.

"I'm very certain that Our Lord didn't say any more to His Apostles through His instructions and His physical presence than He says to us through His good inspirations and His grace. He could have said to St. Peter: 'Ask me for the strength to accomplish what you want.' But no, He didn't because He wanted to show him his weakness, and because, before ruling the Church that is filled with sinners, he had to experience for himself what man is able to do without God's help.

"Before Peter fell, Our Lord had said to him: 'And once you are converted, strengthen your brethren.'** This means: Convince them of the weakness of human strength through your own experience."

LC 140-141 8/7

Scripture

* *"Now Peter was sitting outside in the courtyard. And a maid came up to him, and said, 'You also were with Jesus the Galilean.' But he denied it before them all, saying, 'I do not know what you mean.' And when he went out to the porch, another maid saw him, and she said to the bystanders, 'This man was with Jesus of Nazareth.' And again he denied it with an oath, 'I do not know the man.' After a little while the bystanders came up and said to Peter, 'Certainly you are also one of them, for your accent betrays you.' Then he began to invoke a curse on himself and to swear, 'I do not know the*

man.' And immediately the cock crowed. And Peter remembered the saying of Jesus, 'Before the cock crows, you will deny me three times.' And he went out and wept bitterly."

MATTHEW 26:69-75

** *"Simon, Simon, behold, Satan demanded to have you, that he might sift you like wheat, but I have prayed for you that your faith may not fail; and when you have turned again, strengthen your brethren."*

LUKE 22:31-32

2.
"Little Way"

☩

Scripture

"And they were bringing children to him, that he might touch them; and the disciples rebuked them. But when Jesus saw it he was indignant, and said to them, 'Let the children come to me, do not hinder them; for to such belongs the kingdom of God. Truly, I say to you, whoever does not receive the kingdom of God like a child shall not enter it.' And he took them in his arms and blessed them, laying his hands upon them."

MARK 10:13-16

COME LITTLE ONE

"I understand so well that it is only love which makes us acceptable to God that this love is the only good ambition. Jesus deigned to show me the road that leads to this Divine Furnace, and this road is the *surrender* of the little child who sleeps without fear in its Father's arms. 'Whoever is a *little one*, let him come to me.'"*

SS 188

Scripture

* *"Now they were bringing even infants to him that he might touch them; and when the disciples saw it, they rebuked them.*

But Jesus called them to him, saying, 'Let the children come to me, and do not hinder them; for to such belongs the kingdom of God. Truly, I say to you, whoever does not receive the kingdom of God like a child shall not enter it.'"

Luke 18:15-17

EVEN MORE THAN MY DESIRES

"O my Jesus! what is your answer to all my follies? Is there a soul more *little*, more powerless than mine? Nevertheless even because of my weakness, it has pleased You, O Lord, to grant my *little childish desires* and You desire, today, to grant other desires that are *greater* than the universe."

SS 193

THE ELEVATOR

"We are now living in an age of inventions, and we no longer have to take the trouble of climbing stairs, for, in the homes of the rich, an elevator has replaced these very successfully. I wanted to find an elevator which would raise me to Jesus, for I am too small to climb the rough stairway of perfection. I searched, then, in the Scriptures for some sign of this elevator, the object of my desires, and I read these words coming from the mouth of Eternal Wisdom: '*Whoever is a LITTLE ONE, let him come to me*,'* And so I succeeded. I felt I had found what I was looking for. But wanting to know, O my God, what You would do to *the very little one* who answered Your call, I continued my search and this is what I discovered: *'As one whom a mother caresses, so will I comfort you; you shall be*

77

carried at the breasts, and upon the knees they shall caress you.** Ah! never did words more tender and more melodious come to give joy to my soul. The elevator which must raise me to heaven is Your arms, O Jesus! And for this I had no need to grow up, but rather I had to remain *little* and become this more and more."

SS 207-208

Scripture

* "'Whoever is simple, let him turn in here!' To him who is without sense she says, 'Come, eat of my bread and drink of the wine I have mixed. Leave simpleness, and live, and walk in the way of insight.'"

PROVERBS 9:4-6

** "For thus says the LORD: 'Behold, I will extend prosperity to her like a river, and the wealth of the nations like an overflowing stream; and you shall suck, you shall be carried upon her hip, and dandled upon her knees. As one whom his mother comforts, so I will comfort you; you shall be comforted in Jerusalem.'"

ISAIAH 66:12-13

Prayer

O my Jesus, pick me up in Your arms, too, and be my Elevator to heaven. I want to be with You for all eternity. Amen.

HIDDEN SECRETS

"Often the Lord is pleased to grant wisdom to the little ones, and that one day, in a transport of joy, He blessed His *Father* for having hidden His secrets from the wise and prudent and for revealing them to the *little ones*."*

SS 209

Scripture

* *"At that time Jesus declared, 'I thank thee, Father, Lord of heaven and earth, that thou hast hidden these things from the wise and understanding and revealed them to babes; yea, Father, for such was thy gracious will. All things have been delivered to me by my Father; and no one knows the Son except the Father, and no one knows the Father except the Son and any one to whom the Son chooses to reveal him."*

MATTHEW 11:25-27

LITTLENESS

"I am *too little* to have any vanity now, I am *too little* to compose beautiful sentences in order to have you believe that I have a lot of humility. I prefer to agree very simply that the Almighty has done great things in the soul of His divine Mother's child, and the greatest thing is to have shown her her *littleness*, her impotence."

SS 210

NOURISHMENT

"I threw myself into the arms of God as a little child and, hiding my face in His hair, I said: 'Lord, I am too little to nourish Your children; if You wish to give through me what is suitable for each, fill my little hand and without leaving Your arms or turning my head, I shall give Your treasures to the soul who will come and ask for nourishment.'"

SS 238

Prayer

Lord, I love the image St. Thérèse used of a little child being held in Your arms. Please, dear Father, let me come to You. Hold me. Love me. Amen.

LOWER YOURSELF TO ME

(Couplets composed by Thérèse.)

"You who know my extreme littleness,
  You don't hesitate to lower Yourself to me!
  Come into my heart, O white Host that I love,
  Come into my heart, for it longs for You!
  Ah, I desire that Your goodness would let me
  Die of Love after receiving this favor.
  Jesus! Listen to my tender cry.
  Come into my heart!"

LC 91 7/12

THE LITTLE WAY

"It's the way of spiritual childhood, it's the way of confidence and total abandon. I want to teach them the little means that have so perfectly succeeded with me, to tell them there is only one thing to do here on earth: to cast Jesus the flowers of little sacrifices, to take Him by caresses; this is the way I've taken Him, and it's for this that I shall be so well received."

LC 257 July

A LITTLE SAINT

"No, I don't believe I'm a great saint; I believe I'm a very little saint; but I think God has been pleased to place things in me which will do good to me and to others."

LC 131 8/4

A LITTLE CHILD

(When asked to explain what she meant by "remaining a little child before God.")

"It is to recognize our nothingness, to expect everything from God as a little child expects everything from its father; it is to be disquieted about nothing, and not to be set on gaining our living. Even among the poor, they give the child what is necessary, but as soon as he grows up, his father no longer wants to feed him and says: 'Work now, you can take care of yourself.'

"It was so as not to hear this that I never wanted to grow up, feeling that I was incapable of making my living, the eternal life of heaven. I've always remained little, therefore, having no other occupation but to gather flowers, the flowers of love and sacrifice, and of offering them to God in order to please Him.

"To be little is not attributing to oneself the virtues that one practices, believing oneself capable of anything, but to recognize that God places this treasure in the hands of His little child to be used when necessary; but it remains always God's treasure. Finally, it is not to become discouraged over one's faults, for children fall often, but they are too little to hurt themselves very much."

LC 139 8/6

Scripture

"At that time the disciples came to Jesus, saying, 'Who is the greatest in the kingdom of heaven?' And calling to him a child, he put him in the midst of them, and said, 'Truly, I say to you, unless you turn and become like children, you will never enter the kingdom of heaven. Whoever humbles himself like this child, he is the greatest in the kingdom of heaven.'"

MATTHEW 18:1-4

INFIDELITY

"Oh! If I were unfaithful, if I committed only the slightest infidelity, I feel that I would pay for it with frightful troubles, and I would no longer be able to accept death. Thus I never cease to say to God: 'O my God, I beg You, preserve me from the misfortune of being unfaithful."

(When asked what infidelity she was speaking about.)

"A proud thought voluntarily entertained. For example, if I were to say to myself: I have acquired a certain virtue, and I am certain I can practice it. For then, this would be relying upon my own strength, and when we do this, we run the risk of falling into the abyss. However, I will have the right of doing stupid things up until my death, if I am humble and if I remain little. Look at little children: they never stop breaking things, tearing things, falling down, and they do this even while loving their parents very, very much. When I fall in this way, it makes me realize my nothingness more, and I say to myself: What would I do, and what would I become, if I were to rely upon my own strength?"

LC 140 8/7

Prayer

Oh, so many times I fail. Day after day, I fall short of the life I want to live for You. Continue to give me the strength I need each day to get up and try again to serve You. Amen.

GOD'S VALUES

"It is to God alone that all value must be attributed; there's nothing of value in my little nothingness."

LC 141 8/8

SAINTHOOD

(When told she was a saint.)

"No, I'm not a saint; I've never performed the actions of a saint. I'm a very little soul upon whom God has bestowed graces; that's what I am. What I say is the truth; you'll see this in heaven."

LC 143 8/9

JUDGMENT OF THE "LITTLE" ONES

"As far as little ones are concerned, they will be judged with great gentleness.* And one can remain little, even in the most formidable offices, even when living for a long time. If I were to die at the age of eighty, if I were in China, anywhere, I would still die, I feel, as little as I am today. And it is written: 'At the end, the Lord will rise up to save the gentle and humble of the earth.'** It doesn't say 'to judge,' but 'to save.'"

LC 199 9/25

Scripture
* *"For the lowliest man may be pardoned in mercy, but mighty men will be mightily tested. For the Lord of all will not stand in awe of any one, nor show deference to greatness; because he himself made both small and great, and he takes thought for all alike."*

WISDOM 6:7

** *"Humble yourselves before the Lord and he will exalt you."*

JAMES 4:10

3.
The Trial of Faith

✠

THICKEST DARKNESS

"At this time [prior to Easter Season 1896] I was enjoying such a living faith, such a clear *faith*, that the thought of heaven made up all my happiness, and I was unable to believe there were really impious people who had no faith. I believed they were actually speaking against their own inner convictions when they denied the existence of heaven, that beautiful heaven where God Himself wanted to be their Eternal Reward. During those very joyful days of the Easter season, Jesus made me feel that there were really souls who have no faith, and who, through the abuse of grace, lost this precious treasure, the source of the only real and pure joys. He permitted my soul to be invaded by the thickest darkness, and that the thought of heaven, up until then so sweet to me, be no longer anything but the cause of struggle and torment. This trial was to last not a few days or a few weeks, it was not to be extinguished until the hour set by God Himself and this hour has not yet come. I would like to be able to express what I feel, but alas! I believe this is impossible. One would have to travel through this dark tunnel to understand its darkness."

SS 211-212

Prayer

Darkness is frightening. I can't see You or hear You. Help me remember You're always near me. Amen.

THE FOG

"Then suddenly the fog which surrounds me becomes more dense; it penetrates my soul and envelopes it in such a way that it is impossible to discover within it the sweet image of my Fatherland [heaven]; everything has disappeared! When I want to rest my heart fatigued by the darkness which surrounds it by the memory of the luminous country after which I aspire, my torment redoubles."

SS 213

I WANT TO BELIEVE

"When I sing of the happiness of heaven and the eternal possession of God, I feel no joy in this, for I sing simply what I WANT TO BELIEVE. It is true that at times a very small ray of the sun comes to illumine my darkness, and then the trial ceases for *an instant*, but afterwards the memory of this ray, instead of causing me joy, makes my darkness even more dense."

SS 214

Prayer

Like Thérèse, I want to believe and be strong in my faith. Please shine Your rays of sunshine, Your gentle light, on me when it seems that darkness is everywhere. Amen.

INTERIOR TRIALS

"Ah! the Lord is so good to me that it is quite impossible for me to fear Him. He has always given me what I desire or rather He has made me desire what he wants to give me; thus a short time before my trial against the faith began, I was saying to myself: Really, I have no great exterior trials and for me to have interior ones God would have to change my way. I do not believe He will do this, and still I cannot always live in repose as I am now; what means, then, will Jesus find to try me? The answer was not long in coming, and it showed me that the One whom I love is not at a loss as to the means He uses. Without changing my way He sent me the trial which was to mingle a salutary bitterness with all my joys."

SS 250

TENDERNESS

(After receiving several gifts on the anniversary of her Profession.)

"It's all God's tenderness towards me; exteriorly, I'm loaded with gifts; interiorly, I'm always in my trial *(of faith)* … but also in peace."   *LC 186 8/8*

AT PEACE

"If you only knew the poverty I'm in! I know nothing except what you know; I understand nothing except through what I see and feel. But in my soul, in spite of this darkness … is an astonishing peace."

LC 199 9/24

4.
Charity and Your Neighbor

FORGET MYSELF

"I felt *charity* enter into my soul, and the need to forget myself and to please others; since then I've been happy!"

SS 99

NEW COMMANDMENT

"God has given me the grace to understand what charity is; I understood it before, it is true, but in an imperfect way. I had never fathomed the meaning of these words of Jesus: *'The second commandment is LIKE the first: You shall love your neighbor as yourself.'** I applied myself especially to *loving* God, and it is in loving Him that I understood my love was not to be expressed only in words, for: *'It is not those who say: 'Lord, Lord! who will enter the kingdom of heaven, but those who do the will of my Father in heaven.'*** Jesus has revealed this will several times or I should say on almost every page of His Gospel. But at the Last Supper, when He knew the hearts of His disciples were burning with a more ardent love for Him who had just given Himself to them in the unspeakable mystery of His Eucharist, this sweet Savior wished to give them *a new commandment*. He said to them with inexpressible tenderness: *'A new commandment I give you that you love* *one another: THAT AS I HAVE LOVED YOU, YOU ALSO LOVE ONE ANOTHER. By this will all men know that you are my disciples,* if you have love for one another."****

SS 219

Scripture

* "But when the Pharisees heard that he had silenced the Sadducees, they came together. And one of them, a lawyer, asked him a question, to test him. 'Teacher, which is the great commandment in the law?' And he said to him, 'You shall love the Lord your God with all your heart, and with all your soul, and with all your mind. This is the great and first commandment. And a second is like it, You shall love your neighbor as yourself. On these two commandments depend all the law and the prophets.'"

MATTHEW 22:34-40

** "Not every one who says to me, 'Lord, Lord,' shall enter the kingdom of heaven, but he who does the will of my Father who is in heaven."

MATTHEW 7:21

*** "A new commandment I give to you, that you love one another; even as I have loved you, that you also love one another. By this all men will know that you are my disciples, if you have love for one another."

JOHN 13:34-35

THE LIGHT OF CHARITY

"I saw I didn't love them [sisters in the community] as God loves them. Ah! I understand now that charity consists in bearing with the faults of others, in not being surprised at their weakness, in being edified by the smallest acts of virtue we see them practice. But I understood above all that charity must not remain hidden in the bottom of the heart. Jesus has said: *'No one lights a lamp and puts it under a bushel basket, but upon the lamp-stand, so as to give light to* ALL *in the house.** It seems to me that this lamp represents charity which must enlighten and rejoice not only those who are dearest to us but 'ALL *who are in the house'* without distinction."

SS 220

Scripture

* *"You are the light of the world. A city set on a hill cannot be hid. Nor do men light a lamp and put it under a bushel, but on a stand, and it gives light to all in the house. Let your light so shine before men, that they may see your good works and give glory to your Father who is in heaven."*

MATTHEW 5:14-16

YOUR WILL TO LOVE

"Ah! Lord, I know you don't command the impossible. You know better than I do my weakness and imperfection; You know very well that never would I be able to love my Sisters [sisters in the community at Carmel] as You love them, unless *You,* O my Jesus, *loved them in me.* It is because You wanted to give me this grace that You made Your *new* commandment. Oh! how I love this new commandment since it gives me the assurance that Your Will is *to love in me* all those You command me to love!"

SS 221

ACTING IN ME

"When I am charitable, it is Jesus alone who is acting in me, and the more united I am to Him, the more also do I love my Sisters [sisters in the community in Carmel]."

SS 221

ONE'S RIGHTS

"Ah! what peace floods the soul when she rises above natural feelings. No, there is no joy comparable to that which the truly poor in spirit experience. If such a one asks for something with detachment, and if this thing is not only refused but one tries to take away what one already has, the poor in spirit follow Jesus' counsel: '*If anyone takes away your coat, let go your cloak also.*'*

"To give up one's cloak is, it seems to me, renouncing one's ultimate rights; it is considering oneself as the servant and the slave of others. When one has left his cloak, it is much easier to walk, to run, and Jesus adds: '*And whoever forces you to go one mile, go two more with him.*'* Thus it is not enough to give to *everyone who asks*;** I must even anticipate their desires, appear to be very much obliged and honored to render service, and if anyone takes something which is for my use, I must not appear to be sorry about this but happy at being *relieved* of it … I am very far from practicing what I understand, and still the desire alone I have of doing it gives me peace."

SS 226-227

Scripture

* "*You have heard that it was said, 'An eye for an eye and a tooth for a tooth.' But I say to you, Do not resist one who is evil. But if any one strikes you on the right cheek, turn to him the other also; and if any one would sue you and take your coat, let him have your cloak as well; and if any one forces you to go one mile, go with him two miles. Give to him who begs from you, and do not refuse him who would borrow from you.*"

MATTHEW 5:38-42

** "*Give to every one who begs from you; and of him who takes away your goods do not ask them again. And as you wish that men would do to you, do so to them.*"

LUKE 6:30-31

TO LEND OR TO GIVE

"Our Lord said: '*And if you lend to those from whom you hope to receive in return, what merit have you? For even sinners lend to sinners that they may get back in return as much. But do good, and lend, NOT HOPING FOR ANYTHING IN RETURN, and your reward shall be great.*'*

"Oh yes! the reward is great, even on this earth; in this way it is only the first step that costs anything. *To lend* without *hoping for anything* appears difficult to nature;

one would prefer *to give,* for a thing given no longer belongs to one."

SS 229

Scripture

* *"If you love those who love you, what credit is that to you? For even sinners love those who love them. And if you do good to those who do good to you, what credit is that to you? For even sinners do the same. And if you lend to those from whom you hope to receive, what credit is that to you? Even sinners lend to sinners, to receive as much again. But love your enemies, and do good, and lend, expecting nothing in return; and your reward will be great, and you will be sons of the Most High; for he is kind to the ungrateful and the selfish. Be merciful, even as your Father is merciful."*

LUKE 6:32-36

DON'T DEFEND OR EXPLAIN

"When we're misunderstood and judged unfavorably, what good does it do to defend or explain ourselves? Let the matter drop and say nothing. It's so much better to say nothing and allow others to judge us as they please! We don't see the Gospel where Mary explained herself when her sister accused her of remaining at Jesus' feet, doing nothing!* She didn't say: 'Oh Martha, if you only knew the joy I am experiencing, if you only heard the words I hear! And besides, it's Jesus who told me to remain here.' No, she preferred to remain silent. O blessed silence that gives so much peace to souls!"

LC 36 4/6

* *"And she had a sister called Mary, who sat at the Lord's feet and listened to his teaching. But Martha was distracted with much serving; and she went to him and said, 'Lord, do you not care that my sister has left me to serve alone? Tell her then to help me.' But the Lord answered her, "Martha, Martha, you are anxious and troubled about many things; one thing is needful. Mary has chosen the good portion, which shall not be taken away from her."*

LUKE 10:39-42

NO "THANK YOU"

(With regard to feelings when we have performed a service and received no thanks.)

"I assure you, I too experience the feeling you are speaking about. However, I don't allow myself to be trapped by it, for I expect no reward at all on earth. I do everything for God, and in this way I can lose nothing, and I'm always very well repaid for the trouble I go to for my neighbor."

LC 42 5/9

NO TORMENT

"Whenever I involuntarily caused anyone any trouble, I would beg God to repair it, and then I no longer tormented myself with the matter."

LC 93 7/13

5.
How to Pray

✠

REAL PRAYER

"I was very fond of the countryside, flowers, birds, etc. Sometimes I would try to fish with my little line, but I preferred to go *alone* and sit down on the grass bedecked with flowers, and then my thoughts became very profound indeed! Without knowing what it was to meditate, my soul was absorbed in real prayer. I listened to distant sounds, the murmuring of the wind, etc.… filling my heart with sweet melancholy. Earth then seemed to be a place of exile and I could dream only of heaven."

SS 37

THINKING

"One day, one of my teachers at the Abbey asked me what I did on my free afternoons when I was alone. I told her I went behind my bed in an empty space which was there, and that it was easy to close myself in with my bed-curtain and that 'I *thought*.' 'But what do you think about?' she asked. 'I think about God, about life, about ETERNITY … I *think*!' The good religious laughed heartily at me, and later on she loved reminding me of the time when I *thought*, asking me if I *was still thinking*. I understand now that I was making mental prayer without knowing it and that God was already instructing me in secret."

SS 74-75

Prayer

Dear God, I want to "think," too. I need to slow down during my busy day and make time for You. Whisper Your secrets to me. I'm listening. Amen.

POWER OF PRAYER

"How great is the power of *Prayer*! One could call it a Queen who has at each instant free access to the King and who is able to obtain whatever she asks. To be heard it is not necessary to read from a book some beautiful formula composed for the occasion. If this were the case, alas, I would have to be pitied! Outside the *Divine Office* which I am very unworthy to recite, I do not have the courage to force myself to search out *beautiful* prayers in books. There are so many of them it really gives me a headache! and each prayer is more *beautiful* than the others. I cannot recite them all and not knowing which to choose, I do like children who do not know how to read, I say very simply to God what I wish to say, without composing beautiful sentences, and He always understands me. For me, *prayer* is an aspiration of the heart, it is a simple glance directed to heaven, it is a cry of gratitude and love in the midst of trial as well as joy; finally, it is something great, supernatural, which expands my soul and unites me to Jesus."

SS 242

FATHER

"Sometimes when my mind is in such a great aridity that it is impossible to draw forth one single thought to unite me with God, I *very slowly* recite an 'Our Father' and then the angelic salutation; then these prayers give me great delight; they nourish my soul much more than if I had recited them precipitately a hundred times."

SS 243

Prayer
Our Father

Our Father, who art in heaven, hallowed be Thy name; Thy kingdom come; Thy will be done on earth as it is in heaven.

Give us this day our daily bread; and forgive us our trespasses as we forgive those who trespass against us; and lead us not into temptation, but deliver us from evil. Amen.

6.

Acceptance of God's Will

✠

DEFINING AN ALL-POWERFUL GOD

(As a child, when asked, "How is it that God can be present in a small host?")

"That is not surprising, God is all-powerful."

(And when asked "What does all-powerful mean?")

"It means He can do what He wants!"

SS 27

Prayer

May the all-powerful God guide me and protect me. Amen.

MY CHOICE

"I cried out: 'My God, *I choose all!* I don't want to be a *saint by halves*, I'm not afraid to suffer for You, I fear only one thing: to keep my *own will*; so take it, for *I choose all* that You will!'"

SS 27

OBSTACLES

"In spite of all obstacles, what *God willed* was really accomplished. He *did not allow* creatures to do what they willed but *what He willed.* "

SS 136

TRIAL AND THEN REWARD

"My heart was broken when going to Midnight Mass; I was counting so much on assisting at it behind Carmel's grilles! This trial [to be so ill and not able to serve] was very great for my faith, but *the One whose heart watches even when he sleeps,* made me understand that to those whose faith is like that of a *mustard seed* He grants *miracles* and moves mountains in order to strengthen this faith which is *still small;** but for His *intimate friends,* for His *Mother,* He works no miracles *before having tried their faith.* Did He not allow Lazarus to die even after Martha and Mary told Him he was sick?** At the wedding of Cana when the Blessed Virgin asked Jesus to come to the help of the head of the house, didn't He answer her that His hour had not yet come?*** But after the trial what a reward! The water was changed into wine … Lazarus was raised from the dead! Thus Jesus acted towards His little Thérèse: after having tried her for a *long time,* He granted all the desires of her heart."

SS 142

Scripture

* *"Then the disciples came to Jesus privately and said, 'Why could we not cast [the demon] out?' He said to them, 'Because of your little faith. For truly, I say to you, if you have faith as a grain of mustard seed, you will say to this mountain, 'Move from here to there,' and it will move; and nothing will be impossible to you."*

MATTHEW 17:19-20

** *"Now a certain man was ill, Lazarus of Bethany, the village of Mary and her sister Martha. It was Mary who anointed the Lord with ointment and wiped his feet with her hair, whose brother Lazarus was ill. So the sisters sent to him, saying, 'Lord, he whom you love is ill.' But when Jesus heard it he said, 'This illness is not unto death; it is for the glory of God, so that the Son of God may be glorified by means of it.'"*

JOHN 11:1-4

*** *"When the wine failed, the mother of Jesus said to him, 'They have no wine.' And Jesus said to her, 'O woman, what have you to do with me? My hour has not yet come.'"*

JOHN 2:3-4

Prayer

Be gentle when You test me, Lord. I always want to do Your will. Jesus, smile on me and remind me often that all will be well. Amen.

AT THE MOMENT

"I have frequently noticed that Jesus doesn't want me to lay up *provisions*; He nourishes me at each moment with a totally new food; I find it within me without my knowing how it is there. I believe it is Jesus Himself hidden in the depths of my poor little heart: He is giving me the grace of acting within me, making me think of all He desires me to do at the present moment."

SS 165

A COMPASS

"Neither do I desire any longer suffering or death, and still I love them both; it is *love* alone that attracts me, however, I desired them for a long time; I possessed suffering and believed I had touched the shores of heaven, that the little flower [Thérèse] would be gathered in the springtime of her life. Now, abandonment alone guides me. I have no other compass! I can no longer ask for anything with fervor except the accomplishment of God's will in my soul without any creature being able to set obstacles in the way."

SS 178

Prayer

My Lord, I want to do Your will but sometimes I'm not sure what it is. Guide me! Amen.

SELF-SURRENDER

"Oh! how sweet is the way of Love! How I want to apply myself to doing the will of God always with the greatest self-surrender!"

SS 181

Prayer
I give all my life, everything I say and everything I do, to You with my love. Amen.

AS HE LIKES

"It is only that I feel I have nothing to fear now. In fact, I can rejoice in them, referring to God whatever good there is in me since He has willed to place it there. If He pleases to make me appear better than I am, this is none of my affair since He is free to act as He likes."

SS 206-207

MY SACRIFICE

"My one purpose, then, would be to accomplish the will of God, to sacrifice myself for Him in the way that would please Him."

SS 218

IMPOSSIBLE ALONE

"From the moment I understood that it was impossible for me to do anything by myself, the task you imposed upon me no longer appeared difficult, I felt that the only thing necessary was to unite myself more and more to Jesus and that *'all these things will be given to you besides.'**

SS 238

Scripture

* *"Therefore I tell you, do not be anxious about your life, what you shall eat or what you shall drink, nor about your body, what you shall put on. Is not life more than food, and the body more than clothing? Look at the birds of the air: they neither sow nor reap nor gather into barns, and yet your heavenly Father feeds them. Are you not of more value than they? And which of you by being anxious can add one cubit to his span of life? And why are you anxious about clothing? Consider the lilies of the field, how they grow; they neither toil nor spin; yet I tell you, even Solomon in all his glory was not arrayed like one of these. But if God so clothes the grass of the field, which today is alive and tomorrow is thrown into the oven, will he not much more clothe you, O men of little faith? Therefore do not be anxious, saying, 'What shall we eat?' or 'What shall we drink?' or 'What shall we wear?' For the Gentiles seek all these things; and your heavenly Father knows that you need them all. But seek first his kingdom and his righteousness, and all these things shall be yours as well."*

MATTHEW 6:25-33

SAILING

"There's great peace in my soul … My little boat is sailing once again. I know I shall not return, but I am resigned to remain sick for several months, as long as God wills it."

LC 89 7/11

MY WILL

"God will have to carry out my will in heaven because I have never done my own will here on earth."

LC 91 7/13

Prayer
Lord, St. Thérèse was able to accept Your will for her. Give me the faith and trust I need to turn my life over to You, completely. Amen.

I'LL DESIRE

"God made me always desire what He wanted to give me."

LC 94 7/13

PROFOUND PEACE

"My heart is filled with God's will, and when someone pours something on it, this doesn't penetrate its interior; it's a nothing which glides off easily, just like oil which can't mix with water. I remain always at profound peace in the depths of my heart; nothing can disturb it."

LC 97-98 7/14

REJOICE IN DEATH

"According to my natural inclinations, I prefer to die, but I rejoice in death only because it's God's will for me."

LC 114 7/27

THE FAVOR

"I've never asked God for the favor of dying young; I'm sure, then, that at this moment He's accomplishing His own will."

LC 115 7/ 28

TO BE A MARTYR

"And I who desire martyrdom, is it possible that I should die in bed!"

LC 132 8/4

Prayer
Lord, You know I have made lots of plans for my life, but I want to do Your will. Help me to always know which plans are Yours and which ones are just mine. Amen.

WHAT MAKES ME HAPPY

(After being asked if she would prefer to die soon or to continue to suffer for months or years.)

"Oh! no, I wouldn't be at all happier. What makes me happy is only to do the will of God."

LC 175 8/30

Prayer
Almighty God, I come to do Your will. Show me the way. Amen.

7.

Acceptance of Suffering

✠

BENEATH THE SNOW

(Thérèse is writing in the third person.)

"Ah! if God had not showered His beneficent *rays* upon His little flower [Thérèse], she could never have accustomed herself to earth, for she was too weak to stand up against the rains and the storms. She needed warmth, a gentle dew, and the springtime breezes. Never were these lacking. Jesus had her find them beneath the snow of trial!"

SS 35

TRIALS AND STRENGTHS

"How good God really is! How He parcels out trials only according to the strength He gives us."

SS 47

Prayer
Thank You, Lord, for Your strength in times of distress. Amen.

TO LOVE SUFFERING

(The day after her First Communion.)

"I felt born within my heart a *great desire* to suffer, and at the same time the interior assurance that Jesus reserved a great number of crosses for me. I felt myself flooded with consolations so *great* that I look upon them as one of the *greatest* graces of my life. Suffering became my attraction; it had charms about it which ravished me without my understanding them very well. Up until this time, I had suffered without *loving* suffering, but since this day I felt a real love for it. I also felt the desire of loving only God, of finding my joy only in Him."

SS 79

Prayer

So often I want to run from suffering. I want it to stop. Teach me to embrace my aches and pains out of love for You. Amen.

THE ATTRACTION

"When one wishes to attain a goal, one must use the means; Jesus made me understand that it was through suffering that He wanted to give me souls, and my attraction for suffering grew in proportion to its increase."

SS 149

SPIRITUAL ARIDITY

"My desire for suffering was answered, and yet my attraction for it did not diminish. My soul soon shared in the sufferings of my heart. Spiritual aridity was my daily bread and, deprived of all consolation, I was still the happiest of creatures since all my desires had been satisfied."

SS 157

Prayer

Stay with me, Lord, and comfort me whenever I think You have left me alone. Amen.

INTERIOR SUFFERING

"*'You have given me DELIGHT, O Lord, in ALL your doings.'** For is there a *joy* greater than that of suffering out of love for You? The more interior the suffering is and the less apparent to the eyes of creatures, the more it rejoices You, O my God! But if my suffering was really unknown to You, which is impossible, I would still be happy to have it, if through it I could prevent or make reparation for one single sin against *faith*."

SS 214

Scripture

* "*For thou, O LORD, hast made me glad by thy work; at the works of thy hands I sing for joy. How great are thy works, O LORD! Thy thoughts are very deep!*"

PSALM 92:4-5

PRECIOUS TREASURES

"Suffering itself becomes the greatest of joys when one seeks it as the most precious of treasures."

SS 218

THE CUP WITHDRAWN

"For a long time I have not belonged to myself since I delivered myself totally to Jesus, and He is therefore free to do with me as He pleases. He has given me the attraction for a complete exile and He has made me *understand all the sufferings* I would meet with, asking me if I would want to drink this chalice to the dregs; I wanted to seize this cup immediately when Jesus presented it, but He withdrew His hand and made me understand that my resignation alone was pleasing to Him."

SS 218

Prayer

Jesus, I know You don't want me to suffer just for suffering's sake. And so I accept whatever trials You send to me. I do this as a love offering to You. Amen.

GOD'S AID

"I haven't any misgivings whatsoever about the final struggles or sufferings of this sickness, no matter how great they may be. God has always come to my aid; He has helped me and led me by the hand from my childhood. I count upon Him. I'm sure He will continue to help me until the end. I may really become exhausted and worn out, but I shall never have too much to suffer; I'm sure of this."

LC 50 5/27

THE EMBROIDERY

"I'm reminded of a piece of cloth stretched over a frame to be embroidered; then nobody shows up to embroider it! I wait and wait! It's useless! ... However, this isn't really surprising since little children don't know what they want!

"I'm saying this because I'm thinking of little Jesus; He is the one who has stretched me over a frame of sufferings in order to have the pleasure of embroidering me; then He loosens me so that he can go up to heaven and show them His beautiful work.

LC 64 6/13

Prayer

At the end of my time here on earth, Lord, I hope the embroidery of my life will be rich with the threads of Your love for me. Help me to accept the trials I face. I know that when I reach heaven, then, I will understand why things happened the way they did for me. Increase my trust in You. Amen.

AN INCONVENIENCE

"I have only inconveniences to put up with, not sufferings."

LC 102 7/18

THINKING OF LOVE

(When asked if her suffering prevents her from thinking clearly.)

"No, it still allows me to tell God that I love Him; I find that this is enough."

LC 119 7/30

PRAY FOR THE SICK

"Little sisters, pray for the poor sick who are dying. If you only knew what happens! How little it takes to lose one's patience! You must be kind towards all of them without exception. I would not have believed it formerly."

LC 130 8/3

Prayer
For the sick and dying, especially those who are most in need of Your compassion, I pray to the Lord. Amen.

WITHOUT FAITH

"How easy it is to become discouraged when we are very sick! Oh, how I sense that I'd become discouraged if I didn't have any faith! Or at least if I didn't love God."

LC 132 8/4

I GIVE YOU MY SUFFERINGS

"My little life is to suffer, and that's it! Otherwise, I wouldn't be able to say: My God, this is for the Church;

my God, this is for France, etc. God knows best what to do with these sufferings; I've given them all to Him to do with as He pleases. Besides, it would tire me out to tell Him: Give this to Peter, that to Paul."

LC 133 8/4

I'M NOT ALONE

"I didn't expect to suffer like this; I'm suffering like a little child.

"I would never want to ask God for greater sufferings. If He increases them, I will bear them with pleasure and with joy because they will be coming from Him. But I'm too little to have any strength through myself. If I were to ask for sufferings, these would be mine, and I would have to bear them alone, and I've never been able to do anything alone."

LC 145 8/11

Prayer
It is comforting to know I'm not alone in this world. The suffering and trials are easier to take because You are here with me. Please stay close. I can't do this alone. Amen.

FROM GOD

(When told, "You had a lot of trouble today.")

"Yes, but since I love it … I love everything that God gives me."

LC 148 8/14

COURAGE INCREASES

"God gives me courage in proportion to my sufferings. I feel at this moment I couldn't suffer any more, but I'm not afraid, since if they increase, He will increase my courage at the same time."

LC 149 8/15

PRAYERS

(When told her caregiver was praying for the relief of her suffering.)

"No, we must leave them alone up there [heaven]!"

LC 151 8/17

DOING IT WELL

"I'm suffering very much, but am I suffering very well? That's the point!"

LC 152 8/18

AID FROM OUR LADY

(Shedding tears after a difficult night.)

"I'm perhaps losing my wits. Oh! If they [the sisters in her community] only knew the weakness I'm experiencing. Last night, I couldn't take any more; I begged the Blessed Virgin to hold my head in her hands so that I could take my sufferings."

LC 154 8/19

Prayer

Mother dear, be with me when I'm suffering, in pain, and discouraged. Intercede with your Son for me and ask Him to send me the graces I need. Amen.

THE PRESENT

"I'm suffering only for an instant. It's because we think of the past and the future that we become discouraged and fall into despair."

LC 155 8/19

ONLY NOW

"This isn't like persons who suffer from the past or the future; I myself suffer only at each present moment. So it's not any great thing."

LC 241 8/20

I WILL NOT BE ABANDONED

"I have not yet spent a night so bad. Oh! How good God will have to be so that I can bear all I'm suffering. Never would I believe I could suffer so much. And yet I believe I'm not at the end of my pains; but He will not abandon me."

LC 164 8/23

NOT IN THE LEAST

(When asked if she was sad after so much suffering.)

"Oh, no, I'm not unhappy in the least; God gives me exactly what I can bear."

LC 168 8/25

Prayer

I always heard that "God fits the back for the burden." I know You won't give me more than I can handle, Lord. Please, send me Your grace and Your strength. Amen.

A LONG ILLNESS

(After a comment that Thérèse's sickness had lasted such a long time.)

"Oh, no, I didn't find it long; when it is all over, you will see that it didn't appear long."

LC 170 8/26

WE NEED GOD'S HELP

"How necessary it is for God to help us when we're suffering so much!"

LC 171 8/26

WITHOUT FAITH — DESPERATION

(When someone said, "What a terrible sickness and how much you're suffering!")

"Yes! What a grace it is to have faith! If I had not had any faith, I would have committed suicide without an instant's hesitation."

LC 196 9/22

Prayer

Father, increase my faith and courage especially when my body feels helpless and my heart is at the point of hopelessness. Amen.

A VICTIM OF LOVE

(After a comment that it was frightful to see her suffering.)

"No, it isn't frightful. A little victim of love cannot find frightful what her Spouse sends her through love."

LC 200 9/25

8.

Holiness

✠

SAINTHOOD

"When reading the accounts of the patriotic deeds of French heroines, especially the *Venerable* JOAN OF ARC, I had a great desire to imitate them; and it seemed I felt within me the same burning zeal with which they were animated, the same heavenly inspiration. Then I received a grace which I have always looked upon as one of the greatest in my life because at that age I wasn't receiving the *lights* I'm now receiving when I am flooded with them. I considered that I was born for *glory* and when I searched out the means of attaining it, God inspired in me the sentiments I have just described. He made me understand my own *glory* would not be evident to the eyes of mortals, that it would consist in becoming a great *saint*! This desire could certainly appear daring if one were to consider how weak and imperfect I was, and how, after seven years in the religious life, I still am weak and imperfect. I always feel, however, the same bold confidence of becoming a great saint because I don't count on my merits since I have *none*, but I trust in Him who is Virtue and Holiness. God alone, content with my weak efforts, will raise me to Himself and make me a *saint*, clothing me in His infinite merits. I didn't think then that one had to suffer very much to reach sanctity, but God was not long in showing me this was so and in sending me the trials I already mentioned."

SS 72

Prayer

All you holy men and women, I want to be a saint, but I'm afraid I don't have the "makings" of sainthood. Pray for me to God Almighty. Ask Him to give me the faith and strength I need to live a holy, a saintly life. Amen.

GOD CANNOT INSPIRE UNREALIZABLE DESIRES

"I have always wanted to be a saint. Alas! I have always noticed that when I compared myself to the saints, there is between them and me the same difference that exists between a mountain whose summit is lost in the clouds and the obscure grain of sand trampled underfoot by the passer-by. Instead of becoming discouraged, I said to myself: God cannot inspire unrealizable desires. I can, then, in spite of my littleness, aspire to holiness. It is impossible for me to grow up, and so I must bear with myself such as I am with all my imperfections. But I want to seek out a means of going to heaven by a little way, a way that is very straight, very short, and totally new."

SS 207

Prayer

Lord, I want to be a saint. Show me the way to reach holiness and don't let me be discouraged in my journey. Lord, be with me always. Amen.

TREASURE

"You will be able to say of me: 'It wasn't in this world that she lived but in heaven, there where her treasure was.'"

LC 148 8/12

GOD'S THOUGHTS

(When the comment was made that the caregivers were caring for a "little saint.")

"Well, so much the better! However, I would want God to say it."

LC 181 9/ 3

Prayer

Dear God, St. Thérèse has shared with me her most intimate thoughts. She found a way to serve You by living a holy life, showing You that she loves You every day. I want to read and re-read her words. Her thoughts often seem quite simple, but they are also life-changing. St. Thérèse shared with us her ideas on praying, living with a neighbor, depending on Your gentle graces, and remaining "little." Help me to follow in her footsteps. Remain with me always. I offer my life to You with my love. Amen.

PART

III

Death

I.

Dying

✠

HOW WILL IT END?

(Thérèse writing in the third person.)

"How will this "story of a little white flower" come to an end? Perhaps the little flower will be plucked in her youthful freshness or else transplanted to other shores. I don't know, but what I am certain about is that God's Mercy will accompany her always, that it will never cease blessing the dear Mother who offered her to Jesus; she will rejoice eternally at being one of the flowers of her crown. And with this dear Mother she will sing eternally the New Canticle of Love."

SS 181-182

DAWN OF THE DAY

(Writing in the third person.)

"Ah! don't think, dear Mother, that your child wants to leave you; don't think she feels it is a greater grace to die at the dawn of the day rather than at its close. What she esteems and what she desires only is *to please Jesus*. Now that He seems to be approaching her in order to draw her into the place of His glory, your child is filled with joy."

SS 208

TO DIE OF LOVE

"How sweet and merciful the Lord really is, for He did not send me this trial until the moment I was capable of bearing it. A little earlier I believe it would have plunged me into a state of discouragement. Now it is taking away everything that could be a natural satisfaction in [place of] my desire for heaven. For I no longer have any great desires except that of loving to the point of dying of love."

SS 214

Prayer

At times, Lord, the world seems bleak to me and I become discouraged. Show Your compassion for me and give me strength. Amen.

TO DIE YOUNG

"I never did ask God for the favor of dying young, but I have always hoped this be His will for me."

SS 215

I'M ARRIVING

"I cough and cough! I'm just like a locomotive when it arrives at the station; I'm arriving also at a station: heaven, and I'm announcing it!"

LC 42 5/7

THE LOTTERY

(With reference to her approaching death.)

"I'm like a person who, having a lottery ticket, runs the chance of winning, more so than one who hasn't a ticket; but still the person is not sure of obtaining a prize. So I have a ticket, my illness, and I can keep up my hopes!"

LC 51 5/27

RESIGNATION

(When asked, "Are you resigned to die?")

"Ah!… I find I need resignation only to live. For dying, it's only joy I experience."

LC 58 6/6

Prayer

I know You have a special day planned for my final reward in heaven, Lord. Only You know the day and the hour. Help me be ready when that day comes, today, tomorrow, or many years from now. Amen.

HOW WILL I DO?

"In my childhood, the great events of my life appeared to me as insurmountable mountains. When I saw little girls make their First Communion, I said to myself: How will I do at my First Communion?… Later: How will I do at entering Carmel?… And afterwards: at taking the Habit? at making Profession? At present, it's: How will I do at dying?"

LC 58 6/6

Prayer

We all look forward with anticipation when we approach any new experience. Help me to be ready when the time comes for my final experience on this earth. Help me, Father. I want to do it well. Amen.

COMFORT FROM THE GOSPELS

(When asked, "Are you sad?")

"Oh! no … I drew this from the Gospel: 'Soon you will see the Son of Man seated on the clouds of heaven.'*

"I answered: "When, Lord?'

And on the opposite page, I read: 'This very day.'

"From all this, I learn to be disturbed about nothing, not to wish to live or to die…"

"However, I do want to go!"

LC 59 6/6

Scripture

* *"When day came, the assembly of the elders of the people gathered together, both chief priests and scribes; and they led him away to their council, and they said, 'If you are the Christ, tell us.' But he said to them, 'If I tell you, you will not believe; and if I ask you, you will not answer. But from now on the Son of man shall be seated at the right hand of the power of God.' And they all said, 'Are you the Son of God, then?' And he said to them, 'You say that I am.' And they said, 'What further testimony do we need? We have heard it ourselves from his own lips.'"*

LUKE 22:66-69

AT THE MOMENT OF DEATH

(Hearing a comment that at the time of death there can be distortions of someone's face.)

"If this happens to me, don't be sad, for immediately afterwards I'll have nothing but smiles."

LC 86 7/10

Prayer

When a loved one dies, we have mixed emotions. Someone is leaving this place, going to the next. We are thankful the suffering is over, but now we are face to face with grief. St. Thérèse knew where true happiness is: with You in heaven. Give me faith, Lord. Amen.

JOB

"I repeat like Job: 'In the morning, I hope I'll not see the night; in the evening, I hope no longer to see the morning.'"

LC 135 8/5

Prayer

God, You pick the time. Help me be ready to go. Amen.

WAITING ON THE SHORE

"I'm like a little Robinson Crusoe on his island. As long as no one made any promises, I was exiled, true; however, I never thought of leaving my island [earth]. But behold they told me of the certain arrival of a ship that was to bring me back soon to my country [heaven]. Then I stayed

on the shore, looking into the distance, always looking …
and seeing nothing appearing on the horizon."

LC 136 8/6

TIME TO GO

"The little flower [Thérèse] has lost its root; this will tell
you I'm on my way to heaven. It's because of this that they
[the Blessed Virgin and the Child Jesus] are so nice to me."

LC 140 8/7

DURING THE NIGHT

*(Following a comment by the caregivers that they would be
sad if Thérèse were to die during the night when no one was
with her.)*

"Ah! I find this would be very charming on His part; He
would be stealing me!"

LC 241 8/15

SPEAK FOR ME

"When I say: 'I'm suffering,' you answer: 'All the better!'
I don't have the strength, so you complete what I want to
say."

LC 224 8/21

Prayer
*Thank You, Lord, for all our caregivers. Watch over them and give them
peace. Amen.*

NO FEAR

(When asked, "Would you be afraid to die tomorrow?")

"Ah! even this evening, I wouldn't be afraid; I would only be filled with joy."

LC 176 8/31

TODAY

(Because of her breathing difficulties, someone said she might die that very day.)

"What happiness!"

LC 177 8/31

MY PREFERENCE

(When asked, "Would you prefer to die rather than live?")

"I don't love one thing more than another … What God prefers and chooses for me, that is what pleases me more."

LC 183 9/4

FALLING INTO GOD'S ARMS

(Overhearing a comment that Thérèse was very tired.)

"That's really true, I am! Yes, I'm like a tired and harassed traveler, who reaches the end of his journey and falls over. Yes, but I'll be falling into God's arms!"

LC 191 9/15

Prayer

God Almighty, please be near to me at the end of my journey. Amen.

PREPARED

"Mother Prioress told me that I have nothing to do in order to prepare for death because I was prepared in advance."

LC 191 9/15

MY DESIRE

"I desire nothing on this earth!"

[quickly changing her mind and adding]

"Yes, I still desire something, and it's heaven!"

LC 191 9/17

Prayer

I, like Thérèse, get discouraged sometimes. It's hard to always have faith, especially when I'm in pain. It drains the body and the soul. Please, dear Lord, give me Your graces. At times of pain and suffering, help me to find the peace St. Thérèse found in loving You. When I feel exhausted, give me strength. When depressed, give me hope. When frightened, give me faith. Be with me now and stay with me to the end of my time on this earth.

Like Thérèse, I am tired and I want to fall into Your arms. Amen.

2.
The Thief

DEATH

(Thérèse frequently used the image of the "Thief" when she described her feelings about death.)

"It's said in the Gospel that God will come like a Thief. He will come to steal me away very gently. Oh, how I'd love to aid the Thief!"

LC 6I 6/9

Scripture

"But of that day and hour no one knows, not even the angels of heaven, nor the Son, but the Father only. As were the days of Noah, so will be the coming of the Son of man. For as in those days before the flood they were eating and drinking, marrying and giving in marriage, until the day when Noah entered the ark, and they did not know until the flood came and swept them all away, so will be the coming of the Son of man. Then two men will be in the field; one is taken and one is left. Two women will be grinding at the mill; one is taken and one is left. Watch therefore, for you do not know on what day your Lord is coming. But know this, that if the householder had known in what part of the night the thief was coming, he would have watched and would not have let his

house be broken into. Therefore you also must be ready; for the Son of man is coming at an hour you do not expect."

MATTHEW 24:36-44

"I'm not afraid of the Thief. I see Him in the distance, and I take good care not to call out [to others]: 'Help, Thief!' On the contrary, I call to Him saying: 'Over here, over here!'"

LC 62 6/9

"Whenever I am speaking of the Thief, I'm not thinking of the little Jesus; I'm thinking of the 'great' God."

LC 64 6/13

(When asked if she wanted to die even before her "trial of faith" had ended.)

"Ah! but I really believe in the Thief! It's upon heaven that everything bears. How strange and incomprehensible it is!"

LC 71-72 7/3

(After a comment was made: "You're really happy today; I feel you've seen the Thief.")

"Yes, each time I am sicker I see Him again. But even though I were not to see Him, I love Him so much that I'm always content with what He does. I wouldn't love Him less if He were not to come and steal me away; it's just the opposite. When He misleads me, I pay Him all sorts of compliments, and He doesn't know what to do with me."

LC 75 7/6

(When asked, "Are you afraid? Do you fear the Thief at the door?")

"Ah, less and less ... No, He's not at the door; He's inside! But what are you saying, little Mother [Agnes of Jesus]! Do I fear the Thief! How can I fear one whom I love so much!"

LC 76 7/7

"We are now at July 8, and on June 9, I saw the Thief. If this is the way He acts, He isn't near to stealing me."

LC 237 7/8

(After a doctor's visit when he found Thérèse's health had improved slightly.)

"The Thief is still absent! Well, as God wills it!"

LC 237 7/9

"They [Mary and Jesus] will not make me last one minute longer than the Thief wants."

LC 85 7/10

(When Mother Agnes of Jesus asks "Where's the Thief now?" Thérèse placed her hand on her chest.)

"He's there! He's in my heart!"

LC 109 7/25

> The Thief will come
> And carry me off.
> Alleluia!

LC 123 7/31

"I thought that I should be very good and should wait for the Thief very nicely."

LC 123 7/31

"God has done what He willed to do ... He will come like a thief at an hour when no one is thinking of Him; that's my idea."

LC 124 7/31

Prayer

Dear Thief, will I be ready when You come for me? Will I welcome You? Give me strength so that I won't be afraid. Amen.

3.
Death

✠

GOD IS SEARCHING

"It's not 'death' that will come in search of me, it's God. Death isn't some phantom, some horrible spectre, as it is represented in pictures. It is said in the catechism that 'death is the separation of the soul from the body' and that is all it is."

LC 41 5/1

WAITING FOR MY SURPRISE

"I have formed such a lofty idea of heaven that, at times, I wonder what God will do at my death to surprise me. My hope is so great, it is such a subject of joy for me, not by feeling but by faith, that to satisfy me fully something will be necessary which is beyond all human conception. Rather than be disappointed, I prefer to keep an eternal hope … just to see God happy will be fully sufficient for my own happiness."

LC 43 5/15

ROSES

(When told that it would be very sad when Thérèse died.)

"Oh! no, you will see … it will be like a shower of roses."

LC 256 6/9

SURE SUCCESS

"I don't know when I shall die; I no longer have any confidence in this sickness … I will not be sure of success until I shall have taken the final step and shall see myself in God's arms."

LC 65 6/15

Prayer

To be in Your arms, Father, is truly a successful end to one's life on earth. Be with me now and at the hour of my death. Amen.

THE SUFFERING OF MARY

"The Blessed Virgin held her dead Jesus on her knees, and He was disfigured, covered with blood! You [Mother Agnes of Jesus] will see something different! Ah! I don't know how she stood it! Imagine if they were to bring me to you in this state."

LC 109-110 7/25

MY FIRST EXPERIENCE

"I'm afraid I've feared death, but I won't fear it after it takes place; I'm sure of this! And I'm not sorry for having lived; oh! no. It's only when I ask myself: What is this mysterious separation of the soul from the body? It's my first experience of this, but I abandon myself to God."

LC 188 8/11

4.
The Death of St. Thérèse

✠

THE END

(Thérèse was in significant pain the last two days of her life, and she suffered terribly right up to her death. Mother Agnes of Jesus recorded some of her last words. LC 204 9/30)

"I no longer believe in death for me … I believe only in suffering … Well, so much the better!..."

"O good Blessed Virgin, come to my aid!"

"If this is agony, what is death?!"

"Ah! my God!... Yes, He is very good, I find Him very good."

"My God, have pity on Your poor little child! Have pity on her!"

"O Mother, I assure you, the chalice is filled to the brim!"

"But God is not going to abandon me, I'm sure."

"Never would I have believed it was possible to suffer so much! never! never! I cannot explain this except by the ardent desires I have to save souls."

"Oh! I love Him!"

"My God … I love You!"

(Thérèse died shortly after 7:00 p.m. on September 30, 1897. After her death, Mother Agnes of Jesus said that

Thérèse had a "heavenly smile" on her face and was "ravishingly beautiful.")

Prayer

Dear God, why am I so afraid of death? Is it fear of the unknown? Anxiety about the possible suffering and pain? Concern for the loved ones I leave behind? St. Thérèse had such an acceptance of her illness and her impending death. An excited anticipation. Such faith! How many times have I prayed the Hail Mary, "pray for us sinners now and at the hour of our death"? Grant me peace and serenity when the time comes and I face death. Help me to remember that death is not to be feared. It is to be welcomed. It is the sign that I will soon be united with You, resting in Your gentle arms. I love You, my Heavenly Father. Amen.

PART
IV

Eternity

JOY WITHOUT CLOUDS

"Earth again seemed a sad place and I understood that in heaven alone joy will be without any clouds."

SS 37

EVERLASTING REPOSE

(Referring to heaven as her Fatherland.)

"I return once more to my Sundays. This *joyous* day, passing all too quickly, had its tinge of *melancholy*. I remember how my happiness was unmixed until Compline. During this prayer, I would begin thinking that the day of *rest* was coming to an end, that the morrow would bring with it the necessity of beginning life over again, we would have to go back to work, to learning lessons, etc., and my heart felt the *exile* of this earth. I longed for the everlasting repose of heaven, that never-ending *Sunday* of the *Fatherland!*"

SS 42

REPAYMENT FOR CAREGIVERS

"Happily, I shall have heaven to avenge myself, for my Spouse is very rich and I shall draw from His treasures of *love* to repay you a hundredfold for all you suffered on my account."

SS 64

A NOBLE NAME

"I understood true greatness is to be found in the soul, not in a name, since Isaiah says: 'The Lord will call his servants by ANOTHER NAME,'* and St. John says: 'To him that overcomes I will give a white stone, and on the stone a NEW NAME written which no man knows but the one who receives it.'** It is in heaven, then, that we shall know our titles of nobility. Then shall every man have praise from God.*** And the one who on earth wanted to be poorest, the most forgotten out of love of Jesus, will be the first, the noblest, and the richest!"

SS 121-122

Scripture

* *"You shall leave your name to my chosen for a curse, and the Lord GOD will slay you; but his servants he will call by a different name. So that he who blesses himself in the land shall bless himself by the God of truth, and he who takes an oath in the land shall swear by the God of truth; because the former troubles are forgotten and are hid from my eyes."*

ISAIAH 65:15-16

** *"He who has an ear, let him hear what the Spirit says to the churches. To him who conquers I will give some of the hidden manna, and I will give him a white stone, with a new name written on the stone which no one knows except him who receives it."*

REVELATION 2:17

*** *"Therefore do not pronounce judgment before the time, before the Lord comes, who will bring to light the things now hidden in darkness and will disclose the purposes of the heart. Then every man will receive his commendation from God."*

I Corinthians 4:5

HIS PALACE

"And what shall our happiness be when we receive Communion in the eternal abode of the King of heaven? Then we shall see our joy never coming to an end; there will no longer be sadness of departings … for His *home* will be ours for all eternity …What He does reserve for us is His Palace of glory where we shall see Him no longer hidden under the appearances of a child or a white host, but such as He really is, in the brightness of His infinite splendor!"

SS 129

THE CELESTIAL PAINTER

"I feel how powerless I am to express in human language the secrets of heaven, and after writing page upon page I find that I have not yet begun. There are so many different horizons, so many nuances of infinite variety that only the palette of the Celestial Painter will be able to furnish me after the night of this life with colors capable of depicting the marvels He reveals to the eye of my soul."

SS 189

SWEET SCENT OF FLOWERS

(Thérèse writing in the third person.)

"Well, the little child [Thérèse] *will strew flowers*, she will perfume the royal throne with their *sweet scents*, and she will sing in her silvery tones the canticle of *Love*."

SS 196

Prayer
There are few things as sweet as the fragrance of a rose. Whenever I smell a rose I will think of St. Thérèse and her gift to the King. Help me to someday reach my final goal and stand before that heavenly throne. I will praise and adore my King forever. Amen.

MY WORKS

"I am very happy to go to heaven very soon, but when I think of these words of God: 'My reward is with me, to render to each one according to his works,'* I tell myself that He will be very much embarrassed in my case. I haven't any works! He will not be able to reward me 'according to my works.' Well, then. He will reward me 'according to His own works.'"

LC 43 5/15

Scripture
* *"Behold, I am coming soon, bringing my recompense, to repay every one for what he has done."*

REVELATION 22:12

IN THE PRESENCE OF THE LORD

"After all, it's the same to me whether I live or die. I really don't see what I'll have after death that I don't already possess in this life. I shall see God, true; but as far as being in His presence, I am totally there here on earth."

LC 45 5/15

Prayer

My Lord, I kneel in Your presence today. You are here with me. I can feel Your peace and grace. I know this feeling will be magnified for me a hundredfold when I join You in heaven. Thank You. Amen.

THE ENVELOPE

(Seeing a photo of herself.)

"Yes, but … this is the envelope; when will we see the letter? Oh! how I want to see the letter!"

LC 46 5/20

LIFE

(After hearing a comment that life is sad.)

"Life is not sad! On the contrary, it is very happy. If you were to say: 'The exile [time on earth] is sad,' I would understand you. We make a mistake in giving the name of life to what must come to an end. It is only to the things of heaven, to what must never die that we must give this real name; and, under this title, life is not sad, but happy, very happy!"

LC 265 June

LITTLE FAVORS

"How unhappy I shall be in heaven if I cannot do little favors on earth for those whom I love."

LC 68 6/29

LAST JUDGMENT

"When will the Last Judgment take place? Oh, I wish it were at this very moment! And what will happen afterwards?"

LC 76 7/6

Prayer
I have so many questions about eternity. Oh! The anticipation! Please give me the patience I need to wait for the time You have chosen for me to join You. Amen.

TEARS IN HEAVEN

(Discussing with herself.)
"Oh, certainly, I shall cry when I see God!

No, we can't cry in heaven.

Yes, we can, since it is said: 'And God will wipe away every tear from their eyes.'"*

LC 81 7/8

Scripture
* *"He will wipe away every tear from their eyes, and death shall be no more, neither shall there be mourning nor crying nor pain any more, for the former things have passed away."*

REVELATION 21:4

A TIME OF THANKS

"In heaven, we shall not meet with indifferent glances, because all the elect will discover that they owe to each other the graces that merited the crown for them."

LC 100 7/15

TO LOVE

(When asked what attracts her to heaven.)

"Oh! it's Love! To love, to be loved, and to return to the earth to make love loved…"

LC 217 MID JULY

DOING GOOD ON EARTH

"I feel that I'm about to enter into my rest. But I feel especially that my mission is about to begin, my mission of making God loved as I love Him, of giving my little way to souls. If God answers my desires, my heaven will be spent on earth until the end of the world. Yes, I want to spend my heaven in doing good on earth. This isn't impossible, since from the bosom of the beatific vision, the angels watch over us.

"I can't make heaven a feast of rejoicing; I can't rest as long as there are souls to be saved. But when the angel will have said: 'Time is no more!' then I will take my rest; I'll be able to rejoice, because the number of the elect will be complete and because all will have entered into joy and repose. My heart beats with joy at the thought."

LC 102 7/17

NOT TO REST

"God would not have given me the desire of doing good on earth after my death, if He didn't will to realize it; He would rather have given me the desire to rest in Him."

LC 102 7/18

HIS WELCOMING SMILE

"If God should scold me, even only a little bit, I will not cry. However, if He doesn't scold me at all, if He welcomes me with a smile, I'll cry."

LC 105 7/21

Prayer

I look forward to knowing the happiness waiting for me in heaven. The complete and unconditional love will be overwhelming, and I know I'm going to cry, crying tears of sheer joy. Amen.

THE WHOLE TRUTH

"It's only in heaven that we'll see the whole truth about everything. This is impossible on earth."

LC 132 8/4

IMAGES OF ANGELS

(When told that as she died beautiful angels would come to her in the company of Our Lord.)

"All these images do me no good; I can nourish myself on nothing but the truth. This is why I've never wanted any visions. We can't see, here on earth, heaven, the angels etc., just as they are. I prefer to wait until after my death."

LC 134 8/5

I'M NOT WORTHY

(Sister Genevieve of the Holy Face (Thérèse's sister, Celine) stated: "Do you believe I can still hope to be with you in heaven? This seems impossible to me. It's like expecting a cripple with one arm to climb to the top of a greased pole to fetch an object.")

"Yes, but if there's a giant there who picks up the little cripple in his arms, raises him high, and gives him the object desired!

"This is exactly what God will do for you, but you must not be preoccupied about the matter; you must say to God: 'I know very well that I'll never be worthy of what I hope for, but I hold out my hand to You like a beggar and I'm sure You will answer me fully, for You are so good!'"

LC 221 8/5

Prayer

St. Thérèse used the charming image of a giant lifting a little soul to his reward. I'm not worthy to be lifted into heaven with You, Lord. Forgive me my sins and show me the way to live a life loving and serving You. Amen.

THE HEAVENLY BANQUET

"[There is a Banquet in] heaven where each one will be placed according to his interior merit, where all will be seated at the heavenly Father's banquet. But, then, what a Servant we shall have, since Jesus has said: 'He will come and serve them!'* This will be the moment for the poor, and especially for the little ones to be recompensed amply for their humiliations."

LC 142 8/8

Scripture
* *"Blessed are those servants whom the master finds awake when he comes; truly, I say to you, he will gird himself and have them sit at table, and he will come and serve them."*

LUKE 12:37

RESTING LATER

(After a comment that Thérèse will be tired after visiting with the members of her community.)

"Yes, but when I am up in heaven, I shall take a rest from it all."

LC 149 8/15

NEW LANGUAGE

"Soon I shall speak only the language of the angels."

LC 198 9/24

Prayer

To be with You is my only wish. Today, I come to You and beg Your forgiveness for my many sins. You are so good to me, always kind and compassionate. You love me in ways beyond anything my mind can understand. I love You and I want to show that love to You. It is hard to live in this world, with money, distractions, noise, and evil, and still be able to see and hear You. But, I know all will be well. Please come and be here with me today. I know You want to talk to me and I really want to hear You. So this time is for us, You and me. Alone, just us, together. Whisper Your sweet secrets to me. I am ready to hear You. Come, my Gentle Father, come. Amen.

Special Prayers of
St. Thérèse of Lisieux

ACT OF OBLATION TO MERCIFUL LOVE

Offering of Myself as a Victim of Holocaust to God's Merciful Love

O My God! Most Blessed Trinity, I desire to *Love* You and make you *Loved*, to work for the glory of Holy Church by saving souls on earth and liberating those suffering in purgatory. I desire to accomplish Your will perfectly and to reach the degree of glory You have prepared for me in Your Kingdom. I desire, in a word, to be a saint, but I feel my helplessness and I beg You, O my God! to be Yourself my *Sanctity*!

Since You loved me so much as to give me Your only Son as my Savior and my Spouse, the infinite treasures of His merits are mine. I offer them to You with gladness, begging You to look upon me only in the Face of Jesus and in His heart burning with *Love*.

I offer You, too, all the merits of the saints (in heaven and on earth), their acts of *Love*, and those of the holy angels. Finally, I offer You, *O Blessed Trinity!* the *Love* and merits of the *Blessed Virgin, my dear Mother*. It is to her I abandon my offering, begging her to present it to You. Her Divine Son, my *Beloved* Spouse, told us in the days of His mortal life: "*Whatsoever you ask the Father in my name he will give it to you!*" I am certain, then, that You will grant my desires; I know, O my God! that *the more You want to give, the more You make us desire*. I feel in my heart immense desires and it is with confidence I ask You to come and take possession of my soul. Ah! I cannot receive Holy Communion as often as I desire, but, Lord, are You not *all-powerful?* Remain in me as in a tabernacle and never separate Yourself from Your little victim.

I want to console You for the ingratitude of the wicked, and I beg of You to take away my freedom to displease You. If through weakness I sometimes fall, may Your *Divine Glance* cleanse my soul immediately, consuming all my imperfections like the fire that transforms everything into itself.

I thank You, O my God! for all the graces You have granted me, especially the grace of making me pass through the crucible of suffering. It is with joy I shall contemplate You on the Last Day carrying the sceptre of Your Cross. Since You deigned to give me a share in this very precious Cross, I hope in heaven to resemble You and to see shining in my glorified body the sacred stigmata of Your Passion.

After earth's Exile, I hope to go and enjoy You in the Fatherland, but I do not want to lay up merits for heaven. I want to work for Your *Love alone* with the one purpose of pleasing You, consoling Your Sacred Heart, and saving souls who will love You eternally.

In the evening of this life, I shall appear before You with empty hands, for I do not ask You, Lord, to count my works. All our justice is stained in Your eyes. I wish, then, to be clothed in Your own *Justice* and to receive from Your *Love* the eternal possession of *Yourself.* I want no other *Throne*, no other *Crown* but You, my *Beloved*!

Time is nothing in Your eyes, and a single day is like a thousand years. You can, then, in one instant prepare me to appear before You.

In order to live in one single act of perfect Love, I OFFER MYSELF AS A VICTIM OF HOLOCAUST TO YOUR MERCIFUL LOVE, asking You to consume me incessantly, allowing the waves of *infinite tenderness* shut up within You to overflow into my soul, and that thus I may become a *martyr* of Your *Love*, O my God!

May this martyrdom, after having prepared me to appear before You, finally cause me to die and may my soul take its flight without any delay into the eternal embrace of *Your Merciful Love.*

I want, O my *Beloved*, at each beat of my heart to renew this offering to You an infinite number of times, until the shadows having disappeared I may be able to tell You of my *Love* in an *Eternal Face to Face!*

MARIE, FRANÇOISE,
THÉRÈSE OF THE CHILD JESUS AND THE HOLY FACE,
UNWORTHY CARMELITE RELIGIOUS.
THIS 9TH DAY OF JUNE,
FEAST OF THE MOST HOLY TRINITY,
IN THE YEAR OF GRACE, 1895
SS 276-277

LETTER CARRIED BY SISTER THÉRÈSE ON THE DAY OF HER PROFESSION

O Jesus, my Divine Spouse! May I never lose the second robe of my baptism! Take me before I can commit the slightest voluntary fault. May I never seek nor find anything but Yourself alone. May creatures be nothing for me and may I be nothing for them, but may You, Jesus, be *everything*! May the things of earth never be able to trouble my soul, and may nothing disturb my peace. Jesus, I ask You for nothing but peace, and also love, infinite love without any limits other than Yourself; love which is no longer I but You, my Jesus. Jesus, may I die a martyr for You. Give me martyrdom of heart or of body, or rather give me both. Give me the grace to fulfill my Vows in all their perfection, and make me understand what a real spouse of Yours should be. Never let me be a burden to the community, let nobody be occupied with me, let me be looked upon as one to be trampled underfoot, forgotten like Your little grain of sand, Jesus. May Your will be done in me perfectly, and may I arrive at the place You have prepared for me.

Jesus, allow me to save very many souls; let no soul be lost today; let all souls in purgatory be saved. Jesus, pardon me if I say anything I should not say. I want only to give You joy and to console You.

SS 275

Chronology

✠

January 2, 1873	Born to Louis and Zelie Martin of Lisieux, France
Early 1875	Statement made by Thérèse, "I will be a religious."
August 28, 1877	Mother dies
October 2, 1882	Pauline (older sister) enters Carmel (is later known as Mother Agnes of Jesus)
March 25, 1883	Beginning of a childhood illness (nervous trembling and hallucinations)
May 13, 1883	Cured by the "smile of the Blessed Virgin"
May 8, 1884	First Communion
June 14, 1884	Confirmation
April 9, 1888	Thérèse enters Lisieux Carmel to become Sister Thérèse of the Child Jesus and the Holy Face
October 1888	Approved to receive the Habit
September 24, 1890	Receives the Veil
February 20, 1893	Mother Agnes of Jesus becomes Prioress at Carmel and Thérèse is assigned to oversee the spiritual formation of the new members of the community
July 29, 1894	Father dies following a long illness

December 1894	Mother Agnes of Jesus asks Thérèse to begin writing her memories
September 14, 1894	Celine (closest sister) enters Carmel to become Sister Genevieve of the Holy Face
January 20, 1896	Thérèse gives Mother Agnes of Jesus *Manuscript A*
March 21, 1896	Mother Marie de Gonzague becomes Prioress and Mother Agnes of Jesus steps down
April 2-3, 1896	First symptoms of illness (later identified as tuberculosis)
April 5, 1896	Beginning of what Thérèse called her "trial of faith"
September 8-16, 1896	Writes *Manuscript B* in two parts: 1) a letter addressed to Jesus and 2) a letter to Sister Marie of the Sacred Heart (Thérèse's oldest sister, Marie)
April 1897	Becomes very ill
April 6, 1897	Beginning of notes taken by Mother Agnes of Jesus for *Last Conversations*
June 1897	Thérèse writes *Manuscript C*
August 19, 1897	Receives Communion for the last time
September 30, 1897	Dies shortly after 7:00 pm
October 4, 1897	Buried in Lisieux cemetery
April 29, 1923	Beatified by Pope Pius XI
May 17, 1925	Canonized by Pope Pius XI
October 19, 1997	Declared a Doctor of the Church by Pope John Paul II